FRE WAYS

Lewis Davies was born in Penrhiwtyn.
Freeways won the John Morgan Travel Writing Award.
His novels include *Work, Sex and Rugby*, *Tree of Crows* and *My Piece of Happiness*, which was first produced as a play. Other work for the theatre includes *Without Leave* and *Eating the Fish*. He won the The Rhys Davies Prize for *Mr.Roopratna's Chocolate* and co-edited the short fiction anthology, *Mama's Baby (Papa's Maybe)*.

Lewis Davies lives in Cardigan and is trying to write, publish and fish.

Freeways

Lewis Davies

PARTHIAN BOOKS

© Lewis Davies 1997
All rights reserved
This edition 2002
Parthian, The Old Surgery,
Napier Street
Cardigan SA43 1ED

WWW.Parthianbooks.co.uk

ISBN 1902638 22 0

Typeset in Galliard by NW.
Printed and bound by Dinefwr Press, Llandybïe.

The publishers would like to thank the Arts Council of Wales
for support in the publication of this volume.

British Library Cataloguing in Publication Data.
A cataloguing record for this book is available from the
British Library.

Cover photograph & design *Freeways* by Gillian Griffiths.
With thanks to the Parthian Collective.

Road map of Western United States 1937 published by
Californian State Automobile Association with kind
permission of the Royal Geographical Society, London.
All photographs by kind permission of Gillian Griffiths

Lewis Davies would like to thank the trustees of the John
Morgan Writing Award for the receipt of a travel bursary
which enabled this book to be researched and written.

For Martha

By the same author

"And the concrete road shone like a mirror under the sun."
John Steinbeck

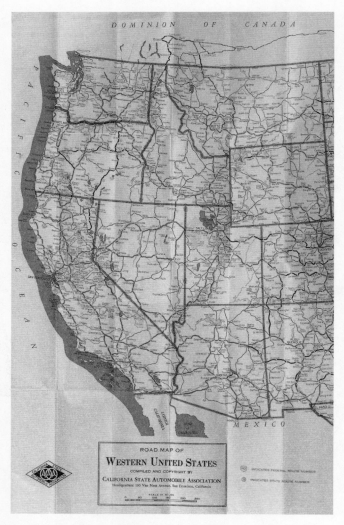

Road map of Western United States, 1937.
Published by Californian State Automobile
Association.
With kind permission of the Royal Geographical Society,
London.

The Road

Used Cars; finance available. The sign promised the key to
the road. The road West. Cash or credit, fill up, drive away,
out of this town.

    The offer was not alone; a whole aerial architecture of
inducements was supported thirty feet above the ground,
vying for space in a scramble for the collective attention with
telephone wires, pizza specials, road signs and traffic lights.
Instruction and warning in a deluge of continuous
communication.

    The man was trying to sell me a Lincoln Zephyr,
avocado green and perched on a ramp at the entrance to his
used lot. Eighteen years old, it looked a bit road-worn,
conscious of the two hundred eighty thousand miles it had
burned along the freeways, enthusiastically contributing to
global warming at fourteen miles per gallon.

    'I'd drive this car all the way to the coast and back, no
problem at all; I know the history on this car.'

    I smiled at him, that must have taken some research. I
was still in High School when the Zephyr rolled off the
production line in Detroit. I touched the wheel, willing it to
tell me some stories.

    'I tell you what, I'd take eighteen hundred cash for this
car right now, let you drive it off the lot.'

    I continued imagining the road ahead. Sal Paradise and
Moriarty belting across the country. Gunning her up; coast

to coast. On the run to the next crazy adventure beneath the skies.

'Insurance, you need insurance ? Insurance is no problem, you've got an Oklahoman driver's license haven't you ?'

I climbed down from the ramp. The car creaked on its blocks willing me to set it on the road again.

In a country entwined in a luxuriant growth of insurance firms, policies, and waivers getting a quote was not going to be a problem; even with a bad driving, debt or bank-robbing record there is always someone to insure you.

'Where you from ?'

'Wales.'

'Where ?'

'It's near England.'

There is a pause as the clerk struggles with his memory. He's heard of it but can't quite place the news report.

'Europe ?'

'Oh sure; you'll need to take a test and written exam.'

'I'm leaving tomorrow.'

The underworld of insurance simultaneously designed to exclude and include. Usually if you're rich you're in; just pay the price. If you're not it depends. I wanted in.

The salesman was disappointed but persistent.

'I'm not saying you shouldn't get insurance, but there's plenty of people out there who don't have it.'

I looked at him as he judged my gullibility. I'm sure he was about to drop the price. Anything to get the Zephyr off the ramp.

'What about the old police car you've got out the back ?'

He didn't speak to me much after that, his enthusiasm gone.

America had arrived in a burst of evening heat and the switching tail-lights of cars on the Freeway. It was a country moving fast and smoothly in the high lingering dusk of a Mid West Summer.

I shared a lift with a lost Texan who had flown in to visit a much missed but long-gone ex-wife. He shifted uneasily in the front seat of the courtesy bus, tired with the flight and the thought of ringing the woman who had moved north to escape him and a restless life in a quiet desert town.

'She sells insurance, farming.'

The woman at the desk is friendly enough and offers to fit me to one of the numerous discounts Econolodge have devised. She decides I could be a student and the Texan a Veteran. We both pay the same thirty-eight dollars. There's breakfast included and free coffee all day.

The motel is cool with a sterility that comes with cheap air-conditioning. The corridors angle off into a ground floor grid pattern that marks my room three doors down from my first travelling partner. He is struggling with the sliding key and is barely controlling his frustration which could be despair. Knowing nothing about sliding door keys, I offer to help. The lock clicks open which surprises me more than the Texan.

'Thanks, perhaps I'll catch you in the morning ?'

He disappears into his room and I take five attempts to open my own.

It's like a set from a bad movie. The sheets are strewn

across the floor, the television is playing to an empty theatre and there is a hanging smell of cheap cigarettes. I look for blood stains and a body.

'Hey, I told the man to clear the room.' The receptionist was embarrassed and annoyed. 'Number seventy-two, third corridor along. Sorry about that.'

The new room is just like the old one but tidier. Thick orange curtains fall down over patio doors blocking my view to the outside world that for tonight is America. The vista is not inspiring: the motel parking lot with only a Dodge pick-up to fill the empty spaces.

I turn the television on and amuse myself with the forty channels. It's such the obvious thing to do, it has to be done. I recognise *Kojak*, *Charley's Angels*, *Star Trek* and then *Tootsie* on one of the movie channels. Then I switch it off.

Sleep is easy as I play games with visions and names of other previous occupants. Faceless stories that are mine only to imagine and therefore easy to let go. One Econolodge room is as likely to be the same as any other.

'I called in.' The Texan struggles with a smile as he sits across from me at the breakfast bar. 'But there was no answer.'

His sentences fragment as he forms them. Words are delivered in slow hesitant gasps which force me to concentrate keenly on what he is trying to communicate.

The waitress arrives as he begins studying the menu. It is a short decision.

'Eggs easy, browns, jelly, coffee.'

The menu is passed back to the waitress who scurries away. It is a type of shorthand that I have already struggled through.

'How would you like your eggs ?'

'Fried ?'

'How ? Side up, over easy ?'

'Er, over easy.'

'Browns ?'

'Eh ?'

The Texan has contacted his daughter as a preliminary. He needed the breakfast to prepare for her mother.

'When I call she usually sees me, but haven't called for six years now.'

His conversation becomes increasingly disjointed but persistent. I try to divert him from his domestic past and imminent future with the knowledge that I'm hoping to buy a car.

'Get a good American car, a Ford or a Lincoln. But not too big; it's a long way to the West Coast. I haven't been there since '87. Had a short job in Sacramento.'

He doesn't elaborate on what he was doing and I don't risk an explanation. I'm struggling with the basics of translation.

He half-offers to come with me to find a car but I deflect the invitation before it becomes too serious. I need to get moving. I finish my third cup of coffee before wishing him luck.

As I leave he is drifting around the foyer watching the phones.

To buy a car I need a car. Tulsa is just too spread out to get anywhere on foot. A high tight skyrise centre collapses to two storeys three blocks out. Space here is not a problem. Who needs to build up when you can build out ?

I arrange a lift back to the airport where I'm promised there will be no problem getting the best deal. The driver works in the kitchen at Econolodge but it's his morning off. He's new in Tulsa, an older brother sponsoring his flight from Bombay and securing a motel job.

'I like it here, this is my country now.'

There were many rules he hadn't picked up yet but he was optimistic.

'This is a good place. Many opportunities but you've got to work hard.'

His young daughter waves enthusiastically from the front seat as her father lets me out at Arrivals.

The airport is open and empty. Last night I presumed it must have been the hour but it's the airport. There is collected lustre to the place that suggests confidence and stable timetables. Catching a flight is easy, just step inside.

There are eight possible hire companies all with their own booths facing in on each other around an arena where the hapless footslogger is surrounded.

I soon find it's not worth the effort shopping around. Prices are matched to each other and Rent-A-Wreck don't run a stand but there is a bewildering array of offers and conditions on specials and discounts : all of which I don't appear to qualify for. I should have pre-booked; I should have a Hertz points card; I should belong to the Holiday Inn Bonus Club. I should have more money.

The cheapest I can scheme is eighty dollars for two days with a bottom of the range Holden. It would have cost sixty-five for one so I thought what's fifteen dollars for an extra day ?

I didn't understand it at the time.

The keys are summoned while I'm asked to sign a sheaf of legal documents and waivers that help keep insurance lawyers the most disliked people in America. I'm finally insured but if I even scratch the car it's going to cost.

The man behind the counter reckons I can get a cheap car on 11th and West.

'It's on Route 66.'

The underground garage is filled with rows of identical silver and grey models attributed to Hertz, Dollar, National Inter Rent and their fellow conspirators.

I try three cars before finding the one my key connects with.

This car's worth more than I've earned in the last ten years and Dollar have given it to me. I crashed the first three cars I owned and incinerated the fourth on Oxwich hill at the height of Summer, causing a traffic jam that simmered back into Swansea. It's amazing what insurance will cover.

A voice welcomed me to the comfort of the interior. Scary.

You know who's in control when the seatbelt automatically straps you to the seat. Never mind automatic transmission - this car runs on computers. I feel like an optional extra some zealous designer reluctantly included as an afterthought.

The cars moves off with various instructions I obediently follow. And now I have to drive on the wrong side of the road. I've spoken to people who claim it's no problem switching sides, straight off the plane straight onto the freeway. Natural drivers, anywhere, any country, any side.

I take three laps of the carpark and two of the perimeter fence before I venture out onto the freeway at forty. Cars overtake me on both sides while I hunt for a route into town.

The speech is smooth and lean, designed to convince me thoroughly of the advantages of buying a vehicle from Cooper's Quality Motors.

'We check these cars thoroughly; each one is cleaned and serviced before we even put them on the stand.'

Bob Wessener has been selling cars for nine months.

'I used to sell insurance but it's kind of dried up right now.' He had drifted into Tulsa for no apparent reason. 'Wife likes it here and I need to keep paying to keep my pension going.'

He had another seven to go but I couldn't see him selling used cars that long. He was out of place in the dull office where the younger salesmen flicked cards across the table at each other on a slow Thursday in the rain.

Despite the stereo "worth a good six hundred" Bob couldn't convince me about the mustard-coloured Ford. It was too big. I didn't want to drive across America in a four-door saloon looking like a family man without the baggage.

The only significant feature of the cars I was being offered as I trudged the used lots on 11th Street was their sheer size. Four litres, eight cylinders, twelve seats, the mathematics multiplied everything into size. Size was obviously a necessary dimension. This is a big continent. We don't go in for any of that economy here, buy American, buy big. Hell, they even make those Toyotas in Kentucky now.

Lee Eller's looked like a used car lot should look like. Big cars, flaking paint, weeds between the tyres and no sign of a salesman. A few flags fluttered in the breeze that dried the pavement into patches.

I peered into the cabs looking for some hints on what I could buy or couldn't afford. Stained synthetic seats, stickers and dust but no prices.

A tall thin guy strides across the forecourt. I think about shuffling away but I'm trapped. He fires a smile at me from twenty feet.

'Mr. Eller ?'

'Mr. Eller's real busy right now but I'm Dick and I'll be mighty glad to help you.'

'I'm looking for a car.'

'Well, we got a few.'

After the third Cadillac I'm beginning to get through to Dick.

'Perhaps you're looking for something smaller ?'

I smile encouragingly.

'Yeh, well you've got to think of fuel economy.'

He leads me beyond the graveyard of fading automobiles that shield Eller's from the rush of 11th Street and the reality of cars that move.

'By the way, where're you from ?' There is a length to his voice that seem to string his words out across his speech extending each syllable as if testing to see if they will snap.

'Wales.'

'That's in Europe, ain't it ?'

'Yeh,' I answer enthusiastically. Someone with geography.

'Is it anywhere near Norway ?'

'Not too far.'

'I've got a friend from Norway, Oslo Norway, Greta. Is that a common name over there ?'

'It is in Norway.'

'Yeh, she's over here in Osteopath hospital, to learn Osteopath medicine.' He imbues her name with a wistful regret that conjures for me sharp green fjords and a Stenna Sealink cashier I once kissed on an Irish Sea car-ferry.

I'm sure he's about to ask me if I know her but remembers that Lee may be watching from the cover of the office blinds and continues into the sales pitch.

'What about the Mustang ?'

It's a good-looking car but it's got a flat tyre.

'It's got a flat.'

'Hey, we can pump that up for you.'

I'm thinking of a way out. There must be another fifty car lots I haven't seen yet. I could drive around them all, check every car and still buy a pig in a barrel.

'There's this Honda just come in yesterday. We haven't cleaned her up yet but she'd sure be good on fuel.'

The Honda might once have been a metallic silver but has weathered to a washed grey smudged with a brown dust that clings to the body suggesting an easy acquaintance with the open road.

'She's a bit high on mileage but there's a great set of tyres.'

The tyres are clean, wide and new and what's two hundred and fourteen thousand miles on a ten-year-old car?

'The Honda Prelude,' he stretches the last three letters of 'prelude' until they merge, 'is a fine car.'

'What about parts?'

'It's Japanese but there's a Honda dealership in every town. Ten years ago you may have had a problem but not now. They're a popular car.'

The car is small and manageable; it looks good. Low, two doors and big tyres. I ask to see the engine because I guess you're expected to when buying a car. The engine looks fine. It's there.

Lee Eller's is an as-seen place. No guarantee. I drive it off the lot and it's mine.

'It's got manual transmission but it's a breeze when you get used to it.'

'It's got a gear-stick?'

'Yeh kind of.'

I think about kicking the tyres but I know you don't need it.

'Can I have a test drive?'

'Yeh sure, I'll just get the keys.'

Dick runs to the office. I guess it has been a slow week.

The car glides low and smooth to the road as I drive into the wide open suburbs that flourish on the north side of Tulsa. Affluence seems to bear a direct correlation to the size of the foliage you can afford in your driveway.

Dick is excited but attempts to play it cool. This could be a sale. We talk terms.

'You're not looking for finance are you ?'

'No, I got cash.'

'Good because we don't do any financing.'

The car is marked for $1700 but I reckon I can get it for fourteen. The speed with which Dick agrees suggests I should have gone lower. I was never very good at buying cars.

ও

The forms needed to hire a car pale against the mesh of paper needed to buy one. Dreams of cash down and drive away fade into Thursday evening. Dick can't find a few that I need to sign. The office is as worn as most of the cars on the lot. A jigsaw print of the Eiffel Tower hangs from one wall, the Taj Mahal from another, glass fronted and cut into a thousand pieces each.

'You like the pictures. Mr Eller does them in the slow periods. Kinda cheers up the place.'

'Yeh you could say that.'

The phone rings, throwing Dick into confusion as he isolates the one of three phones which wants to talk to him.

'Excuse me a minute. My sister.'

Mr.Eller arrives when it's time to hand over the money. He's short, overweight with a colouring that suggests he's been drinking too many Bourbons. He doesn't look like a man who devotes himself to jigsaws in his spare time.

'That's a good car you've got there. I tell you when you get to the West Coast put it in the paper and you'll get your money back.'

He smiles at me between adding the fifty-dollar bills and pulls on a cigarette.

The smoke rises up through the blades of a dusty fan hanging from the ceiling.

ॐ

Friday evening in sunshine and it's Mayfest in Tulsa. The city's streets are thronged with people peering into booths at a fair. It has a small town on holiday feel of candyfloss and watercolours.

The scale is human. All the tents and wooden booths have been put up the day before and will be gone again by Sunday. The huge skyrise, empty and gorged with space, provides a structure to the streets but appears irrelevant to the people entrained within the fair.

I buy a wooden yo-yo for no reason.

ॐ

I linger on the outskirts of Tulsa for three days. There's no rush to get moving and I've no route other than to head west. The city is built on a bluff above the banks of the Arkansas river that will eventually merge with Mississippi a long way to the south east.

I spend an hour looking for the Tourist Information Center but it's been blown away by a hurricane and I've missed it by a Summer. It didn't appear that they had any plans to replace it.

Mid Sunday morning I stumble over the grounds of the Oral Roberts University attracted by a pair of forty-foot hands clasped in prayer over the tree-filled campus. The name registers from a burst of news reports when Oral claimed he'd been ordered personally by God to raise $25 million to keep the University going or he was going to be called home. A sort of productivity incentive.

I enter the visitor center ready to laugh. It doubles as a prayer tower and is designed like some leftover from a Sci-fi movie in the 'fifties. You can ring it up and ask for prayers to be paged for a sick aunt or ailing husband.

I'm ushered into a movie theatre by a serious-looking young man in a suit. His blond hair is cropped close and he speaks in a hushed, reverent whisper.

I'm expecting a sales pitch about the glory of evangelism but it's a simple history of the University contrasting its measured progress in education and missionary work against the conflicts of a wider America from the 'fifties to now. Images of Vietnam and student protest clashed with the calm of Tulsa. Each still image had its own accompanying soundtrack. The campus had always been fully integrated. It had no history of student unrest. It seemed the ideal place to learn for committed evangelists.

After twenty minutes the show closed. I felt as if I'd been entertained. Oral Roberts University seemed okay but the rest of the world had a better soundtrack.

Picking up 66 again on the edge of Tulsa I head south towards Oklahoma City. The car feels good on the road as the stop-lights thin and suburbs stretch into farmland.

The Sixty Six motif appears on old motels and new signs in a succession of small towns that live in the flow of the Highway as it ages into America's mobile heritage.

It's a figure that sticks in the memory, enmeshed in the expanding tendrils of mass culture and eulogised in song lyrics and movie scripts. The towns that fringe the road hang onto the route as a grip on their own history.

I pass a string of visitor centers, original 66 Diners and curio shops before finally being persuaded to stop an hour short of the State Capital.

'I been up and down this road all my life, hell I'm part of the junk in here.' Henry Southers was running the Chandler 66 which boasted an authentically rusting collection of signs, petrol pumps, water buckets, and license plates in addition to a bewildering array of moulded plastic objects and stickers with the accompanying logo.

'Business is good, there's a preservation society in Oklahoma now, opened a big museum down near Elk City, got stuff you'd never imagined existed. The things people get attached to on this road. But be careful there's a big trade in fakes.' He winked, suggesting that he wasn't above passing one or two himself.

I picked my way through the wreckage of the store trying not to disturb the dust or become entangled in the thicket of paint-flaked metal. A brace of neon signs hung lifelessly above a battered typewriter on a wooden shelf.

'It's from the 'thirties.'

The road first cut through the State in the Summer of 1926 as part of the first National Highways programme. A

Tulsa businessman called Cyrus Avery convinced a Congressional Committee of a route that dipped down from Chicago, Illinois pushing through the center of Oklahoma on to New Mexico, Arizona and finally meeting the Coast at Santa Monica Pier in California.

Within a decade it had entered an American consciousness that associated the road West with a dream of opportunity and prosperity. It was the road to the coast.

'My granddaddy helped to build it then ran across to California when the work dried up around here. Didn't last too long out there though. Think he came back just after the war. My father reckons it was a beat-up little road then and he didn't like the sight of the plains one bit when he was brought back home. Hadn't seen it before 'count of him being born over there. Me of course I was brought up around here but we used to go on road trips down into the South West. Went all the way over to Albuquerque once. It was starting to fade then but now it's coming right back into style with the movies an' such.' He waved an arm expansively over the mass of his accumulated stock.

'Yes, there's a lot of interest in the road now, even the old movies and all those films like the *Grapes of Wrath*.'

For John Steinbeck chronicling the flush of migrants into California during the Depression Storms of the 'thirties it provided the ideal metaphor to begin the flow of his book.

'Sixty Six is the path of a people in flight, refugees from dust and shrinking land, from the thunder of tractors and shrinking ownership, from the desert's slow northward invasion, from the twisting winds that howl up out of Texas, from the floods that bring no richness to the land and steal what little richness is there. From all these the people are in flight, and

*they come into 66 from the tributary side roads, from the wagon
tracks and the rutted country roads. 66 is the mother road, the
road of flight.'*

He was recording the uprooting of a people and their
push westward along a road that had been substantially
constructed with money from New Deal projects. Money
intended to shore the collapse of an an ailing economy used
to construct a road that became an escape for thousands of
people abandoned by that same economy.

For much of the 'thirties it was a road of flight but with
the end of World War II prosperity returned to America,
emphasised by an explosion in motor-car ownership and
Route 66 became another symbol; a symbol of a prosperous
country on the move with money to spend. The lure of the
Coast was still there but people began to head west just for
the thrill of the road.

'Course it's changed but there's a lot of people with
more time on their hands for touring, older folks like me
who remember it like it used to be and don't mind taking
their time crossing the country. And we get a lot of tourists
through here. Germans are real interested in it for some
reason. Get a few every week.'

Jack Kerouac was just one of thousands of tourists
moving across the continent in huge cars burning cheap
petrol while supporting a huge infrastructure of garages,
diners, and motels that fringed the highway waiting for the
dollars to drive by.

66 became the main street of America, a road of drive-
ins, motor lodges and refrigerated air that created a
mythology to survive beyond the construction of the larger
faster freeways in the 1960s.

The new roads bypassed the small towns that had depended on the highway for their survival while near the cities, franchise chains offered a monotonous standard of comfort and taste that had become necessary. Who wanted to watch black and white television when the chains had colour ? Many of the businesses collapsed or changed form as travel became faster moving beyond the flow of the journey. But the road was patient and waited.

'I used to sell insurance but no go after the oil market slumped thought it was a good time to get into this instead. I like this; people are happy when they walk out of here. Bought something they wanted. Not like in insurance if you know what I mean.'

Despite the growth of air travel most Americans still travelled by car and with age came nostalgia. Memories of a first trip West, real or imaginary, focused attention again on the route of the Mother Road. History and mythology conspired to hold onto a strip of the past.

The Heritage road is now a reality.

'Sure I can't interest you in anything else? It'll be a long way to come back.'

Oklahoma City straddles Route 66 near the center of the State. I arrive late and pitch into a grubby hotel just off Lincoln Boulevard. The rooms are cheap but they couldn't charge any higher.

Drouth Survivor

Tulsa University has an art gallery named after a painter
called Alexandre Hogue. I turned up on a hot Sunday
morning in May. It was closed until Monday. I hung around.

By Monday it was open but there was no sign of any
paintings by Hogue. Big modernist canvasses and a piece of
installation art in a wide dark corridor. No one around. The
University looked vacant, scattered among the oak trees in
suburban Tulsa as if afraid and hiding from the students.

I finally flushed a secretary. She must have been in early.

'We have one, in here.' She led me into a cluttered
paper-strewn office. Half-hidden by a filing cabinet a framed
severe sketch in pencil. Self Portrait, Alexandre Hogue.

A gaunt severe man stared out at me from within the
portrait, a gaze forty years old.

'Perhaps you should try the Philbrook, it's open
tomorrow.'

I'd been in Tulsa five days. It was time to move on.

Hogue had raised his reputation out of the dust bowl
with stark hyper-realist canvases of the effects of the storms
and poverty which forced so many people to flee West in the
'thirties. It was a fascination with the death and decay of the
small farms he had known and loved as a kid that he
transferred to his work. It was a fascination that did not
endear him to frustrated civic authorities who thought his
work portrayed the affected areas unfavourably.

The citizens of Dalhart, a town badly affected by the storms and economic decline which spread over the panhandle, even made a collection of fifty dollars and sent an emissary to Dallas where an exhibition of his work was being held. The idea was to buy the canvas Drouth Survivors, return with it to Dalhart and then burn it ceremonially in the town square. The plan failed. The painting was for sale at $2000.

I had liked the story. Two thousand dollars must have seemed a lot of money for a painting when your farm or business was failing for want of a few hundred.

Two days later I was searching the fairgrounds in Oklahoma City for another gallery. White and red redundant rides spread over twenty acres waited for the Summer weekends. I wondered about the money required to keep a place this big going in the off-season. I guess not much rusted in the Mid West. The cars were thirty years old.

I had to pay to get in the gallery. I prefer free exhibitions but there was a reduction for students.

'I'm a student.'

'You really ? What type of student ?' The man was earnest and enthusiastic. I was struggling.

'Art student.'

'Really, you're over here studying Art ?' I guess he'd gauged my accent.

'Kind of.'

'Anything in particular ?' His eyes were gleaming. Poised, eager to help. I was feeling a fraud.

'Mid Western, sort of depression era.'

'You mean the Labor Works Programme artists.'

'Er yeh, got any ?'

'Well I'm not sure, but Brian, he'll know. He's on

lunch right now but as soon as he's back I'll bring him over. You have a look around.'

'Great, thanks.'

'That'll be two dollars sixty.'

'I haven't got any ID.'

He smiled and waved his hand. 'That's fine.'

I ambled around the gallery for twenty minutes. An eclectic mixture, sharply realist to pure abstract. The gallery was wide and light with a confusing circular corridor that guided me around to the entrance again when I thought I should have been at least a block away.

I was making a second circuit when Brian arrived.

'Hello, I'm Brian.' He shook my hand warmly. 'You're studying the Works Programme artists?' He was as earnest as the first man but even more friendly, eyes beaming behind wire spectacles.

'Anyone in particular?'

'Alexandre Hogue, but I couldn't find any of his work.'

'Hogue, you say.' He quickly placed the name. 'No I don't think we've got any out at the moment, but may have one in the stores. I think we have.'

He led me back down towards the entrance of the gallery. He was from Oklahoma City but had once spent an unhappy week in Bangor.

'I was due to start at the University, but it didn't work out.'

'One week?'

'My landlord was just horrible, still.' There was a regret lingering in his words.

'You could have changed digs?'

'Perhaps it wasn't for me.'

He unlocked a door into a large open storeroom. Three

rows of paintings stacked in vertical shelves lined the far wall. Years of work; thousands of dollars facing the wall in a storeroom.

He searched along the rows, checking the typed labels stuck to the back of each canvas.

'Here it is.' He pulled out a large canvas. Bright with Hogue's reds and greens of enhanced realism. A gully in the panhandle. Water levels low, soil erosion, no people. There's a collapsed barbed wire fence supporting a sign with sun-bleached letters spelling Posted. It's the ruin of a dream.

'It's the only one we have, I'm afraid.' He was genuinely disappointed. 'The Philbrook in Tulsa will have more.'

Tulsa was three days behind now. I didn't want to drive back.

'Of course you could always call in to see him, I'm sure he'd talk to you.'

The implication in the speech caught me by surprise. I was looking at the work of a man who had come to prominence in the 'thirties. I was looking at the work of a dead man.

'He's still alive ?'

'Well yes.' My surprise seemed to shake his certainty. 'I think so.'

The work was from another era. The men and women I'd been searching for were all long gone. Steinbeck, coronary failure in the 'sixties. Woody Guthrie, a long slide to death from Huntington's Chorea. Dorothea Lange buried in an Oakland churchyard. All safely dead and the subject of long scholarly biographies. The longevity of Hogue stirred a sharper perspective.

'I'm sure he lives in Tulsa. I'll see if I can find him in

the phonebook.'

He disappeared into a side office while I looked at the painting again.

'He wasn't in the book but I got him through enquiries.' He handed me the number.

It was strange. Just ring somebody out of the past I'd already buried him in.

A woman entered the storeroom from the main door into the gallery.

'Hi Brian ?' She was loud and then louder. Obviously used to being the center of attention, she sauntered to where Brian and I were looking at the picture. She was the boss.

'Who's this guy ?'

Brian quietly explained who I was and why I was in the storeroom.

'Hogue eh ?' She stared at the picture. 'Not very interesting is it ?'

'I've just found his phone number, he's still living up in Tulsa, he thinks he might call to see him.'

'Still alive eh? Must be well into his nineties by now, guess you won't get much out of him, he'll be dribbling everywhere.'

I just wanted the woman to go away. I looked at her blankly. She seemed to sense she was not going to be the center of attention for much longer. It made her feel uneasy.

'Well, good luck with the vegetable.' She sauntered back out. Brian shook his head slowly and we silently agreed not to discuss her.

'I'll get you a picture of it.' He retreated back into his office before returning with an instant camera, then carefully positioned the frame in the best light. He clicked and we watched as Hogue's gully in the panhandle coloured on the celluloid.

'Good for the research.'

Geary

I head into Geary early on a bright Thursday morning, a breakfast stop on the route up into the Oklahoman panhandle. The low clouds that shrouded Tulsa have been blown away, revealing a deep blue sky of no definition.

Geary is a slow, farming town that looks as if it has retired. I share a greasy breakfast in a pre-fab on the edge of town with a bunch of old farmers in cowboy hats.

I try to catch the drift of their conversation but I'm a table too far away and the voices are disjointed. It's a real parliament; everyone appears to want an opinion. They leave in groups of two and three and I chance a word with one of the stragglers.

'You'll have to speak up son, my hearing ain't what it used to be.'

He peers up at me through sharp grey eyes. He is almost bald and was alone in not wearing a cowboy hat. Stubborn grey bristles push out from his lined skin. An audio aid bulges from his ear.

After the third attempt I scribble "hello" on a scrap of paper followed by "I'm from the U.K.".

'Good.'

He gets up and walks to the counter to pay his bill. The waitress smiles at me as the man exits the door.

'He's a bit deaf.'

I park the Honda near the crossroads at the center of town attracted by a painted window that informs that the contents within are part of the town's historic museum.

It is staffed by the diners with whom I shared the Breakfast bar. I am their first visitor of the day and there is a debate about who will show me around. Finally Ed wins the argument and embarks on the guided tour of the old shoeshop on the corner of Main and 1 which now served as the town's museum and a social center for its older residents.

The room is stuffed with enduring ephemera: Indian blankets, an old photograph of Jessie Chisholm, civil war muskets and WWII naffy tins, a 'fifties coffee machine. Some of the staff had probably stocked the shelves by turning out an attic.

Ed is a retired farmer.

'Sold out twenty years back now. Bin a long time doing nothing.' He chuckles at his own joke. 'My brother reckons this is the biggest run of foolishness I've ever put my mind to, says it should all be forgotten.'

He waits for my reassurance but still seems unconvinced. A growth of doubt planted by his brother that he is unable to grub out.

'You're a writer ?'

'Yeh, I'm just sort of passing through right now.'

'What you written ?'

I throw him a title. I know there's not the slightest chance he's heard of it.

'Can't say I've read it.' He pauses as if he's trying to re-thread his thoughts, there was something he was going to say. He looks around uneasily before peering towards me.

'We used to have a writer right here in Geary, disabled feller name of Kent Ruth, real nice, missed him though. He's been dead two years, ever read any of his stuff ?'

'Don't think I have.'

'Real nice, used to live up on Main and Four, house is open if you're interested ?'

'Open ?'

'His sister left the house to the town as a sort of memorial to Kent, we keep it open.' He looks over to the entrance where a couple of women talk easily with each other. 'What time is the Ruth house open ?'

'Eleven ?'

'What was that ? Did you get that ?'

'Eleven.'

'Well yeh, I was saying, I grew up with Kent, always been a cripple but a nice man. Wrote a lot of books, about the West and such, travelling around in a Dodge pick-up. Died a few years back and his sister left the house to the town. We keep it going for anybody who comes through. Just like this place.' He turns nervously to see how far his wife is away at the counter before leaning toward me. 'My brother reckons this is the biggest run of foolishness I've ever set my mind to, reckons we're wasting our time, all this stuff should be thrown away where it belongs ?'

I sign the visitors' book at the counter on the way out. I'm the third tourist of the week but the Museum has swirled with people all morning.

The Ruth house fronts directly onto Main. A wooden picket, one story. Mown grass, bleached paint, sun shutters and rose gone to dog trailing a trellis.

There's a welcoming committee.

'We were just going to lunch, but since you've come all this way we can hang on a while.'

The house feels as if someone is still living in the next room. A patterned settee, china ornaments on the window sill, a full bookcase.

'Kent sure did a lot of reading.'

A copy of *For Whom The Bell Tolls* catches my attention. They don't seem to mind me picking it up. A first edition, I guess how much it is worth. I think of Kent confined to his chair reading of Hemingway and the Spanish Civil War. Different lives.

'Relatives from Oklahoma City took a lot of the books away and some furniture, we haven't gotten around to sorting it yet, need to catalogue it.'

I'm guided through to the study and the atmosphere changes. The front room was B movie 'fifties America, the study is Ruth's. A broad desk peers out through Indian shutters to a shaded orchard. There are still pens on the desk and a pile of business cards, scraps of notepaper, dictionaries. This is not a theme museum; they just haven't sorted the place out.

'We need to throw out a lot of stuff, all his sister's clothes are still in the wardrobe. Need to send them along to the Army stores. Just getting the time, there's only the three of us.'

A couple of his books are still on the desk; several editions are still for sale.

I picked up one bearing the simple title *Touring the Old West*. Kent had arranged to have it reprinted, a couple of years before his death, by the University of Nebraska.

He had written out of his self-professed love for the West, a West of old half-remembered migrant trails and abandoned mining towns, Indian encampments and weathered headstones in townless graveyards. Places he searched out or stumbled across with the help of his sister Helen, a lifelong companion who actually drove their Dodge pick-up around the twenty-one States covered by the book.

The book had come soon after his retirement as a travel editor on the *Daily Oklahoman* and covered thirty years of touring. A reprint followed fifteen years later.

He ends his dedication of the book, '*To Helen who shares a love for the Old West and whose actual touring of it has made our exploration junkets possible and doubly enjoyable.*'

'That'll be nine dollars ninety-five.'

I slip a business card from the desk into the book as a mark. Something personal.

I drove on. The road continued to rise north-west as I climbed into the panhandle following the valley of the Canadian river. Towns floated past, just names. Greenfield, Seiling, Sharon.

Late afternoon was Woodward. I stopped for coffee in a diner that had been run for thirty years by Mabel and George. A plaque on the door paid for by friends commemorates the anniversary.

The waitress guesses I'm from out of town and sits

opposite me while I drink.

'Mabel don't like me talking too much to the customers but it's slow this afternoon.'

She was from Woodward, about my age and lived a few blocks away with her young son and a husband who sold fertiliser.

'Been working here six months, it's friendly but slow, you know what I mean?'

A man in a red check shirt and a huge gallon hat took a seat deeper in the diner.

'Got to get back to work, guess I won't see you around again.'

The State Park was a low-key early season place. A few RV's hooked up between the trees; old folk watching the afternoon slip by. The swimming pool dry, waiting for repair and the Summer.

Three fat men were pulling roach out of the pond; live bait intended for ten-pound catfish that hid in the Canadian river. One of the anglers pulls a record of a successful night, a picture of thirty fish, bloated and lifeless on the back of his pick up.

'The river's thick, never clear them out,' in response to my unvoiced question.

I shared the cheapest pitches on a rough piece of grass under the trees with one other solitary camper.

There didn't seem anything to do but talk to him.

Jameson Doyle was escaping one American dream for another. Eight years as a computer broker in New York had worn the city out of him. Long hours, long flights, two weeks holiday a year. He'd sold up, bought a four wheel drive, a mountain bike and was heading for the Rockies.

'Colorado probably. I spent a week there two years ago, the pace is different.'

He talked quietly by the light of a gas lamp that pulled in every flying insect on the park. He was leaving the East for good, leaving a big money job and the pressure of New York.

'I've had two dates in eight years.'

This was an attractive-looking guy with money. What the hell did you have to do in New York ?

He'd been on the road for ten days. Taking his time gently easing west. Looking for a rhythm of travelling that would lead to a new place. Long rides in the afternoon on his bike. He seemed to be enjoying the freedom.

Jameson was not a slacker. Coupland's treatise on Generation X mid-twenties crisis America didn't seem to fit. He had probably earned more money than his parents ever did. But he was certainly a migrant. America is still full of people running. People on the move to somewhere else. To the hills, to the coast, to the desert. Perhaps the size of the country forces them on.

Coupland had seized the attention of a media desperate for something to write about with a tale of middle-class America opting out of salaries, career structure and pension plans while slacking by on a diet of McJobs, soft drugs and 'seventies music but refusing to move out of a comfortable existence with mom and dad at home.

But every generation has a fringe that rejects it while

the sensible majority push on with the ladder. The fringe gets the publicity and the fun for a while; the sensible people are patient and get the money. Still Generation X had a new angle on it even if it did involve living with their parents.

'There was no rebellion, just a chance to be lazy.'

But Jameson was moving. A big move west on the strength of a well-remembered vacation a couple of Summers ago.

'I need something more and perhaps it's in Boulder.'
We agree to meet at Black Mesa.

I had seen Boise City coming. Sixty miles out across the panhandle, three domes rising out of the ironed flatness marked something. The road ground on; telegraph wires tracing a line into a distance of wheatfields turning to scrub. Nodding donkeys sucking money out of the mantle, while the wheat waited for rain or the vast mobile irrigators that ploughed a straight furrow through fields fifty hectares from fence to fence.

It was these thin sandy soils that faded quickly to dust in the early 'thirties. When a young Associated Press reporter wired New York that the farming belt of the Mid West had become a dustbowl he was constructing a term that would hang to the land and come to underline a decade of brutal change.

The storms of aeolian dust had been flourishing for five or six years encouraged by a series of parched droughts but it was the publicity in the East that broke the story of thick clouds that choked waterways, suffocated cattle and filled hospitals with people dying quickly from swollen lungs. It was a storm that had been building for a generation when an incessant greed for land had pushed farmers out into increasingly marginal areas, borrowing heavily to finance machinery and the cultivation of wheat on thin, drought-ridden soils.

They were filled with the optimism of the American dream and the availability of private capital willing to finance the continued push of manifest destiny. In the great land rushes of the 1890s more and more Indian land was consumed in the greed to cultivate the open prairies in Oklahoma, Texas and Arkansas. The life was never easy with families living poverty-driven lives on the very edge of communication and in constant conflict with the wind and fickle rain of the Mid West.

But there was optimism and it was this optimism that was relentlessly winnowed away with a series of severe droughts in the early 'thirties. There had been storms before, characterized by sharp winds that blew up from the South but they had usually been swallowed by a wet Winter. The frequent storms that cut through the panhandle drifting the loose soils into dunes persisted for a decade. In 1935 Boise City recorded over five hundred hours of storm including the huge Black Dusters which periodically ran through town.

When George Greenfell headlined the *New York Times* in 1936 with the claim he had seen "the cold hand of death on what was one of the great bread baskets of the nation" he was imbuing an Easterner's drama into the practical farming lands but the people had already begun to move, giving up on one dream in trade for another. An exodus was beginning again on the road West.

A shattered house on a rise invites me to stop. There's a persistent wind blowing up from Texas fifty miles to the south. A rough track from the road is littered with the cracked bounty of an abandoned home. Crockery, old and shattered. Pans, twisted out of shape sinking into the soil. Metal pieces, rusted beyond recognition from machines that I can't picture. Objects abandoned in a rush to leave a little house on the hill. There is always too much to carry.

The wind stirs movement from the house; wood swinging on a loose nail, fragments of curtain brushing against an open window. This can't be a duster's house but a feeling of rushed abandonment stains the walls and the cracked plaster.

The families who moved in the 'thirties just walked out. Giving up on the interminable debts and constant droughts. Their houses remained for years like lonely ghosts trapped to the prairie but the people had gone. Boise City lost half its population in a decade as cars and wagons were loaded high with possessions and pushed hard across New Mexico and Arizona following Route 66 while dreaming of prosperity in the golden land on the coast.

Many were not running from farm failure but they were all wound up in the debt of the depression and they had a new dream. A dream fuelled by movement, rumours and boosters that promised jobs at good wages in California. The reception they received would be very different.

Pigeons wheel out of the loft as I climb into a back window. The doors are all boarded but the windows speak with the wind. Thick piles of pigeon shit litter the lino; the birds finding a safe roost on the open prairie.

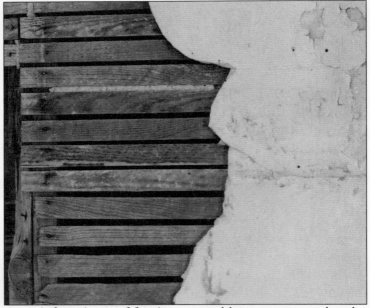

A few pieces of furniture crumble to wormwood and a wood stove has rusted into the back wall.

I touch the decay.

The storms, stories.

The road continues dead west.

By the time I cut into the fringe of town even the tireless evangelist on the radio has resigned himself to the isolation of Boise City. It's out there.

It appears as a town on the high out of nowhere. It was shackled to one of the last areas of freestate in the Union; sitting in a corner of land bordered by Texas, Kansas, New Mexico and Oklahoma, it had no claimants and cultivated a reputation for lawlessness and a last refuge for desperate men on the run. The wide dusty streets still emanate an air of desperation. But now it's only desperation, Oklahoma spoiling the fun when it finally owned up to its responsibility.

There's another town museum but it's closed and an antique shop selling garage sale rejects. A café with a sign promises cooking as good as Grandma's only grandma never could cook.

I sit on a bench outside the town hall. It has a curious fame attributed to tourism brochures and I'm sure it's been used in a movie but I can't remember the title. There's a paper lying on the concrete under a bin. I flick through it casually, there's a lot of farming articles and a piece on the forthcoming hunting season. I read the obituaries. I like obituaries in small town papers; they're kind of sad and reassuring. There's a picture of Franklin Mason who had died aged eighty-seven in Bakersfield, California. He'd left the town in 1932 and his family had written East in case any of his old friends still remembered him. He had fond memories of a youth on the banks of the Cimarron river.

The town's beacon on the plain prove to be wheat and milo silos. A repository for some of the continued wealth that is still ploughed out every season. The droughts faded towards the end of the 'thirties and land quickly regained its stability while the farmers who remained bought up huge acreage at depression prices. The silos mark the headwaters of one of the lines feeding the Santa Fé Railway running down to the main conduit at Albuquerque.

Everything out of here heads west. I rush on to Black Mesa where I'd arranged to meet Jameson.

The evening stretches out alongside another campground. A shallow lake shelters in the lee of an escarpment. A curiously flightless goose waddles along the shoreline stopping hopefully at each campsite. Public information signs give brief histories of the recent past.

Jameson has spent the afternoon on his mountain bike. The time appears to weigh heavy on him.

'I just can't get used to not having to be anywhere. You're the only appointment I had today.'

We spend the evening talking in the glare of his hurricane lamp. As the suns fall a choir of frogs wells up from the lake filling the park with a rough chorus.

'I've read three books since I started. That's one a week. I hadn't read a book in years.'

He lends me the latest one he's finished and gives me an album by The Grateful Dead. The book is *Blue Highways* by William Least Heat Moon; it's about packing in a job and hitting the road. Least Heat Moon is apparently not his real name, but his Indian name. His real name is William Trogdon.

'You can give it back to me if I see you in Taos.'

Jameson continues enthusiastically with more stories of his one holiday in Colorado that is the focus of his new life.

'This town had a giveaway clothes shop. Just a sign saying "free stuff".'

The camp-warden stops briefly to check our permits. I ask about the lone goose.

'Used to have two but some bastards barbecued the other one.'

A tall wire fence runs along the first long road in New Mexico. Short stubby canyons break with the flatness of the prairie and scattered ridge of the Sangre de Cristo Mountains, merge with a heat haze in the distance. It is mid-May but there is still a fall of snow on the high peaks.

I slow the car to watch a Mule Deer that runs parallel to the fence. The animal doesn't seem interested in me but looks for a break to vault the fence and cross the road to an identical open prairie beyond. There a stag shepherds three hinds away from the intruder on the wrong side of the fence. The fence is eight feet high and there are no breaks but the stag looked keen.

I swerve to avoid a land turtle that stalls on a run across the road.

Further on the openness of the land is cruelly contained by the bleakness of a feed lot cattle station. For miles the grazing land is strangely empty; hectares of grassland without a domestic grazer. Then a stench that fills the air with the sodden sadness of five thousand animals closed in open pens and fed with synthesised protein. It's cheaper this way; farmers can now raise cattle by tender in these huge concentration camps that dot the prairie like stagnant cankers. The animal becomes purely a product to be processed and packaged, like any other, to be beyond recognition.

The cows stand knee-deep in shit and urine. The price is not what it costs. American meat is cheap.

Taos

49 KFM plays Bootleg Dylan as the road twists down through the pinewoods of the Sangre de Cristo Mountains into Taos. It's a town that has survived the 'sixties idealism, spent the 'seventies on a spiritual binge before getting real and commercial in the 'eighties.

It's still a small hippy town of sorts but McDonald's has crept up to the stoplights that mark the center of the Mexican quarter. A tree-shaded square with chairs and live music provides a focus for a flock of art galleries and curio shops that have found a niche in the dusty brown adobes.

Taos has been known as an artist's town since the 'twenties when an infamous socialite called Mabel Sterne moved her salon from Greenwich Village and the galleries still turn a brisk trade in dollars from wealthy tourists on a day out in the mountains from Santa Fé to the south. The town is full of painters and sculptors vying to fund a living or find an expression.

Late May and it's mid-season between the Winter skiers and the Summer art-collectors. Trade is slow but a clear blue sky promises warmth as the sun attempts to spirit the last runs of snow from Wheeler Peak, which rises high over the town.

A café bar off the square that doubles as a bookshop serves the best coffee I have tasted on the road. Of course it is also the first not to offer unlimited free refills.

I share the café early on a Sunday morning with a tourist from New York. He is using two of his ten days a year holiday to make it a long weekend in New Mexico.

'You mean you get all this time off to come over here ?'

'I'm sort of working.'

'Yeh sure, find it pays ?'

'This time.'

He lives in Greenwich Village and has undoubtedly come for the art and perhaps the gay scene.

He's reading a book by Robertson Davies and is surprised when I say I've read him. He begins to rhapsodise about the man's erudition but stops abruptly when I suggest I didn't find the author interesting. I can't really remember why I hadn't liked his work so I make something up. Too involved? It's as if I've insulted a close personal friend. He mumbles something about not understanding anything before abruptly leaving the café.

I return to my newspaper.

The bookshop specializes in D.H. Lawrence memorabilia and writings. A whole room devoted to the works and speculation on a man who turned up here by chance in 1922 and a few years later for good. There's a collection of his paintings hung in a hotel in town guarded by a jealous owner who boasts he's turned down a million dollars for them and charges $3 a viewing. The Lawrence ranch is out of town.

Galleries follow the road out competing with expensive restaurants and curio stores selling saddles and sculpture. Dark red touching burgundy chillies swing from the store fronts in huge sheafs emphasising the Mexican past and present of the town.

Further on there's a sign for an Indian Pueblo, with a promise of daily tours organized throughout the Season. I drive up but I've missed the last tour of the morning. The pueblo walls of distinctive honey-brown sunbaked mud protect the interior from prying tourists who are not allowed to walk around unaccompanied. It's just another way of making a living.

Taos proclaims itself as the cultural capital of the Pueblo Indians, many of whose villages still remain hidden away in the New Mexico hills where they trace a history from the Anasazi, who moved up from the south a millennium ago. A man waiting at the gate recommends I should try Sky City.

'If you're going that way past Albuquerque it's one of the best.' He returns to loading film into an expensive camera.

The numerous Indian peoples lasted a long time in New Mexico, even managing to scalp a State governor in 1847. His house is another of the Taos museums.

I rejoin the main highway heading north out of town. The division is quick as commerce recedes quickly into scrubland dominated by the blaze of the mountains. Ten miles out another sign guides me right to the D.H. Lawrence ranch. The surfaced road gives up and a rough gravel track climbs steeply into the forest.

The ranch appears out of the pines, wooden and bleached by the sun; it is owned by the University of New Mexico and run as a study center but there's no sign of any students.

When Lawrence first visited Taos the ranch was owned by Mabel Sterne, who was sustaining a well-earned reputation as a fearsome patron of the arts in addition to developing a new interest in the culture of the Pueblo Indians. On reading Lawrence's *Sea and Sardinia* she became convinced that he was a man able to connect with the Indians' deep mysticism and to convey its qualities to the world through his work. She wrote to Lawrence, offering to finance his stay with the hope of developing an artistic collaboration.

She had the personality and financial independence not to care what people or society thought of her and was already an infamous figure in Taos, having seduced a well-known, charismatic Pueblo Indian named Tony Luhan, who became her fourth husband.

Lawrence and Frieda arrived in the late Summer of 1922, having travelled to the West Coast from Europe via Sri Lanka and Australia. His tuberculosis was deepening despite his own repeated denials of its existence and he was recovering from the effects of a malarial attack while visiting friends in Kandy. The Tropics had not been kind to him. He was still travelling and consciously rootless. Taos was to become his only permanent home since he had been hounded out of Cornwall as an alleged enemy sympathiser in the war-infected Winter of 1917.

Lawrence loved the area immediately and instinctively, *'In the magnificent fierce morning of New Mexico one sprang awake, a new part of the soul woke up suddenly, and the old world gave way to the new.'*

But Frieda was suspicious of their new host's flattery and tired of the succession of women who were drawn to Lawrence's growing reputation as a mystic. Within two months they had decamped to a ranch higher in the mountains, driven by Mabel's excessive demands on his time and attempts to seduce his spirit. Attempts he found particularly repellent.

'I feel I could kill and that I should enjoy doing it. I will kill Mabel first. I will use a knife. I will cut her throat.'

They remained friends.

When not under her pervasive influence Lawrence settled to the Sangre de Cristo Mountains, wintering in the company of a pair of itinerant Danish painters and, the following Summer, using it as a base to venture further south into Mexico. But despite the thin dry mountain air popularly prescribed for tuberculosis sufferers his health continued to decline, along with his marriage to Frieda.

Separating briefly, Frieda returned to London in the Summer of 1923. Lawrence followed her but, detesting London, abandoned the city to return again to Taos in March 1924. This time they bought the ranch, Frieda exchanging the manuscript of *Sons and Lovers* for a run-down collection of shacks which Lawrence named *Lobo* then *Kiowa*. It was here that the many threads of his life were beginning to knot.

Again he was subjected to the powerful demands of Mabel, whom he portrayed brutally in his short story, *The Woman who rode Away*, a harsh tale of a society hostess who, on despairing of her superficial existence, takes to the mountains in an attempt to divine some meaning in her life from the Native Indians. In the final scene she is portrayed prostrate and naked under a huge ice phallus about to be sacrificed as an offering to a fertility god. Lawrence took his revenge in print and imagination seriously but his constant conflicts with Frieda and the other powerful women who had a habit of appearing in his life seeped malignantly into his writing. It was at this time he used his journeys into Mexico to complete *The Plumed Serpent*. He was still writing his life directly into his work but the reality of his illness was closing and, after a severe haemorrhage during a long malarial-plagued visit to Oaxaca, he returned broken and desperately ill to regain a brittle health for a final Summer at Kiowa.

Lawrence left for Europe in the Autumn of 1925 and struggled on in declining health until finally succumbing after a harsh Winter in the town of Vence in the Maritime Alps. But his connection with Taos had not ended.

After his death Frieda needed support to establish her rights to Lawrence's work. There was a bitter court case with Lawrence's family before she was able to return to New Mexico. She owned the ranch but needed a lover to share it with. Her new escort was to be an ex-Italian army officer called Ravagli whom she had seduced from his wife and bought out of service. In 1935 Ravagli, under Frieda's directions, returned to Europe, had Lawrence's remains exhumed, cremated and then shipped to Taos where they were incorporated into a shrine built on the Kiowa ranch they now shared. Frieda joined him twenty years later. Ravagli sold the ranch, the remaining manuscripts, the paintings and went home to Italy.

The sun is shaded from the tomb by a thick growth of

young pines. A blue jay cackles beyond the high branches. A trickle of earnest tourists struggle up the winding path from the ranch. The visitors' book is thick with short deeply-felt eulogies to the dead man. Spirituality is a word that keeps appearing, awakening another. I can remember a week's read and a month's imagining of *Sons and Lovers* while I talked escape with a girl walking through the closed oakwoods of a Welsh mountain.

I keep crossing trails of Lawrence around the world, France, Sri Lanka, Australia, Cornwall, and I wonder what kept him wandering. The rootless outsider, beyond the industrial world he had grown from but never accepted in the tight circles of lettered London until after he no longer cared.

The deep gash of Rio Grande gorge twisted on the bare plain to the south. A hummingbird sucked nectar from a flower the colour of blood. He'd come a long way for a miner's son from Nottingham.

The Rio Grande at sunset. The name echoes from a hundred cowboy films. John Wayne and faceless other actors chasing Apaches and Mexicans across a shallow river. Saturday nights in with my gran while she knitted woollen sweaters; my grandfather drinking whisky and water.

I'm heading out. Three days in Taos and I drive south to pick up the Santa Fé Trail. I stop to buy some food from the K-mart on the edge of town. It's one of those American supermarkets where you can buy everything you ever wanted and didn't need. Huge stacks of food. Everything is in big sizes.

People are ambling around: easy time weekday afternoon in the slack season. The snow on the peak has edged further up since Saturday. Summer begins to be impatient.

A man in ragged clothes offers to clean my windscreen.

'Only a dollar, I'll do a fine job ?' He holds up a plastic bottle flushed with a pale blue detergent. In his other hand a dirty cloth.

'Work's kinda slow this time of year.' His long grey hair is matted and bunched into a pony tail. There is a four-day growth of white stubble but a wide smile still places him younger than he might be.

'I'm a painter but there's nothing going right now. This kinda keeps me busy.'

I imagine an undiscovered talent starving on food stamps while wild flowing masterpieces gather dust in a caravan on a trailer site.

'Houses mostly. But anything that comes up.'

He continues smearing dust around the glass on the Honda.

'Yeh I used to travel about, bin all over New Mexico, Arizona. Came over from the West in the 'seventies, the bubble kinda burst.' He chuckles at his own metaphor.

'Sort of settled down here now. Nice place to stay as long as I can get some work. Pick pecans in November but they don't pay you shit.'

He leans back gauging how much cleaner he can get the windows.

'Hard work and you work for nothing, sometimes I get down as far as Las Cruses, usually something I can do down that way but this country's nice. I've sort of settled right here.'

He thanks me politely for the work before ambling off to the next customer. I'd asked all the questions.

To Walk

Driving up in the panhandle I pass three signs that warn me not to pick up hitchhikers as they may be escaped criminals or inmates. Possibly both.

I shift nervously in my seat thinking of Rutger Hauer in *The Hitcher*. Lonely men on the highway. *The Rough Guide to America* considers hitchhiking a quick route to an unusual suicide. Distrust is everywhere.

The implication is clear. Anyone without a car, without the moving metal emblem of America, belongs outside. A person on the fringes; no friends, no money, no hope. Or maybe they're insane. Who in their sanity is going to walk? It's ninety degrees and a hell of a long way to nowhere.

Even the literary hero of the hitcher was no bum with his thumb out on the road. His alter ego, Sal Paradise, in his first attempt at freeriding finds himself marooned for nine hours on a turnpike in Upstate New York. A thunderstorm eventually forces him to give up and catch a bus to Chicago.

Later Paradise manages to free-ride to Denver but the real hero of *On The Road* was the car. Big six-litre Fords and Cadillacs, guzzling cheap fuel as they gunned from coast to coast. The interior, the vast expanses of Mid West farmland

and Western Desert, was immaterial to the real quest of the crossing. The land just drifted by as a thousand miles and small towns on the highway.

Kerouac talked about people receding on the highway as the cars surged on 'The too huge world vaulting us, and it's good bye. But we lean forward to the next crazy venture beneath the skies.'

When Travis walks out of the desert in Wim Wender's *Paris, Texas* the concern of his brother is not that he has resurfaced after being missing for four years but that he has walked. The fact that he refuses to speak and affects a glazed look confirms his madness or, as it turns out, a trauma. Personal and universal. It is this trauma of loss that saturates the empty towns on the highway where the past is so new and the future is moving too fast away.

Further out along the freeways I occasionally pass a lone man walking. Not hiking or attempting to solicit a lift, just walking along the edge of the road.

I gaze as I pass, intensely curious for a reason. Why is he out there ?

To walk is not to be part of America.

The road cut steeply down the valley keeping pace with the Rio Grande as it surged south to divide Texas from Mexico. A lone turkey vulture soared above the highway looking for road kills. I drive halfway to Santa Fé before pitching up for the night in an Indian-run State park. They're selling licenses to fish for trout in a damned lake but the evening's too still for fishing.

There's a list of thirty regulations to control visitors and fishermen. The lake is surrounded at ten feet precisely demarked intervals by cool-box-sustained anglers throwing flashing spinners into still water. I watch for twenty minutes but the fish are keeping low, nervous of the aerial bombardment that scatters ripples across the lake.

As the sun drops, barbecue smoke fills the campsite, glowing fires feeding on pine and charcoal.

Leaving early, I cut around Santa Fé. I don't feel I need another town stuffed with art galleries and boutiques. A Mexican diner run by white Americans serves great ranch-style eggs. The food from here gets hotter. It's on the edge of the desert where they exploded the first atom bomb and the owner tells me of an abandoned mining town that's worth a visit. A pair of collared doves jostle in a wicker cage. A cockerel with feathered feet pecks in the dust waiting for me to throw it a tortilla. The road's quiet. The restaurant slow. The waitress suggests the same mining town.

'It's a real ghost town, thirty miles or so, on the Turquoise Trail.'

Songlines

As the roads switched and merged, continually pushing on, following valleys or riding high across bleak plateau, older trails pushed up on the map or were marked by newer signs on the highway. The Chisholm cattle trail, the Oregon Wagon trail, the Cimarron cut-off. All marking a journey across the land. The first trappers and traders and later the prospectors and farmers were isolated on a huge, unreadable continent. A land which for them was without map or memory. The older lines that for centuries had been evolving quietly and certainly were useless to the new people.

The trails became the first lines across a new land. These trails were used then taken over by new routes writing new lines, the Santa Fé line and later the roads, Route 66 and then Interstate 40. New routes, faster lines for the new communication. The older trails merging with the land to form heritage pieces. The memory becomes important so you can read the past in lines.

At Madrid I imagined a town that grew out of a mining boom a hundred years ago and became a strictly-controlled company affair providing steam coal for an expanding railway network. During World War II it was sustained by military efforts to construct the bomb at the Los Alamos Nuclear Laboratory but after the war, with the increase in oil production and switch to diesel on the railways, the coal trade slumped. People drifted easily on to another job in the prosperity of post-war America leaving a road fringed by wooden houses that weathered well in the dry desert air.

The early 'sixties saw the town on a coast-to-coast traveller's route and, tiring of the road and liking the clear skies, people began to stay. Squatting in the empty houses still owned by the company, the road became the sound of cars passing through. Selling jewelry and junk that gradually changed to art, the town carved a living again. Today the houses have been bought at auction and the travellers exhibit through smart galleries in Santa Fé and Albuquerque.

George Manus welds sculptures from discarded mine machinery; his metal spiders and grotesque rusting birds advertise themselves and fetch high prices in Santa Fé. He started putting them together for fun in the early 'seventies.

'Sorta helped me understand myself better, they tend to reflect what mood I'm in at the time.'

A huge threatening eagle with bulging eyes bears down on visitors to his open-air gallery.

'Yeh, some people don't like them much but what the hell.'

The coal mine is now a museum and there's an annual opera festival in the Mine Shaft Tavern. Curio shops sneak in on the fringes. I pick my way slowly through the attractions. The sun is warm and the people friendly.

'I'm running the place for my daughter, you should talk to her, she's writing a book on Madrid.'

Towns change quickly in America. One year a boom, the next everything's closing down, people moving on to the next place for the next twenty years of a life. The roots are shallow in a thin soil. People seem to be searching for somewhere to stay but that place is never here. It's easier to accept change in the transience of movement.

I head on.

Over the mountain is Albuquerque.

Whales to America

'You from Whales ?'

He was pronouncing the h.

'Wales, no h.'

'Right, Wales.'

I smiled at him.

'Isn't that boy Jones from over there ? Todd ? Ted ?'

'Tom.'

'That's the boy Tom Jones, does a bit of singing up in Vegas, not a bad singer that boy, he's from Whales.'

There's a Welsh playwright called Ed Thomas who's depressed that when Ian Woosnam won the U.S. Masters he was asked what part of Scotland was Wales in. Wales doesn't exist as far the U.S. is concerned. But then England is only a few minor royals and a couple of actors who occasionally do well at the Oscar Ceremonies. The special relationship the deluded ravings of an attention-seeking Prime Minister. America has difficulty getting interested in the next State never mind the confused and changing geography of a Europe an ocean away. Publicity needs a war.

World affairs rarely make the news if there is no direct American interest. Haiti was a complicated Gulf issue where the media had difficulty in distinguishing between genuine refugees and a boatful of men paddling madly to the land of prosperity. Throw yourself overboard and there's an American coastguard ready to transport you to Miami.

'Hey are you from Ireland ?'

Identity in America is the past. If you have one.

The KOA in Albuquerque is a short drive from the center of town. The Kampground competes for space with industrial estates and DIY superstores. It's a sort of halfway staging post across the continent, the right place to break down. The area is saturated with garages willing to leap on the smallest mechanical fault.

The site has all the facilities required of a Kampground of America; swimming pools, a hot tub, laundry and tv rooms, free coffee. This is not roughing it. It is full of retired people roaming the continent in RV's or recreational vehicles. Forty years of prosperity and high pension returns has created a class of retired gypsies who cross the continent in a belated attempt to see some of it.

The RV's are huge six or eight wheelers up to fifty feet long that loom along the bigger highways. Inside there are double bedrooms, fitted kitchens, living rooms with satellite tv. On top there are usually boats, bikes and barbecue sets for outdoor living while most will pull a smaller car along in their wake for getting around while they're hooked up to a site for a couple of days.

Stickers on the windshield recall journeys and state parks all around the continent as they follow the Seasons. The South for Winter; Summer in the Northern States and into Canada. They're all planning the big one to Alaska. Everything is a possibility.

Albuquerque is for spares and repair.

The tent site is in the far corner of the precisely demarked field. I share a pitch with a retired couple from Denmark. They arrive tired and hot in the early evening after a walk from the center of town. They're bussing it around the States and tried to walk from the terminal. It has taken them three hours.

As night sweeps up from the south-east I take a drive along Route 66 which cuts through the center of the city. The road has attained a heritage feel with neon signs advertising hotels that haven't changed since the height of traffic on the route in the 'fifties. Names like the De Anza Motor Lodge, Chihuahua Charlie's and The Aztec Motel vie for attention and trade. Mexico and a Spanish American history is only across a fluctuating border.

In the morning I offer the Danish couple a lift to the bus station but the husband insists they must get used to the local buses. His wife looks disappointed.

Acoma

I drive out up nine-mile hill looking for Sky City. This time I'm determined to be on time for the tour. The desert is flat and open, then fragments into a series of canyons and harsh dry plains.

Acoma survives as the capital of the Pueblo Nation on an isolated mesa some four hundred feet above the surrounding plateau. It marks the site of the first permanent settlement of the area and, when the Spanish first arrived in the mid 1600s on their long search for gold and heathens, they found a well-developed system of agriculture and a religion they wanted to convert.

Tourism is well-organized. A new visitor center strictly controls admission to the village. Tours leave every half hour and they are all guided along a fixed route where visitors are besieged to buy an overpriced selection of pottery at every open window. Photographs are extra. The old adobe buildings of mud and brick still support some families but most have moved to new houses on the plain below.

'We have cable tv,' the guide informs us twice.

I'm the youngest on the tour by a good thirty years as the shuttle transports us to the top of Acoma.

'They put the road in when they shot a movie here in the 'sixties. It's a popular location.'

There are deep views across the reservation from the summit. It was settled due to a well that holds during the severest droughts. The Indians converted to Catholicism and the ever pragmatic Spanish didn't seem to mind the incorporation of a few rituals into the services. A huge church was constructed on the summit that still fills on festival days.

The graveyard is littered with cracked pots marking the sites of old and new graves as centuries of death pile on each other.

Our group is directed onto another show of pottery which is especially praised as the craftsman is the guide's uncle.

'You are welcome to touch and buy.'

One of the group is about to take a picture of an old woman. She is offering a grotesque ceramic owl with one hand and holding a Seven Up can in the other. The photographer has seen the angle, contrast between the old and new, traditional crafts in a contemporary society. He frames the shot.

'Hey you want to take a picture of Grandma? It'll be ten dollars.'

The camera is put quietly away.

Gallup

Beyond Albuquerque, half-way to Arizona, is Gallup. Stretched along the original National Highway Route 66 between the semi-retired Santa Fé line and the new powerful Interstate 40 it is a town waiting for someone to pass through.

The main strip is fringed by the railway and littered with motels that fade back into the 'fifties like old clothes abandoned on a washing line. Prices are cheap; they have to be. Closer to the edges the newer national chains have tightened the town's resources further. People on the road need never stay in town; the rooms are standard. You know what you're paying for.

But Gallup manages to survive. There's a good deal of traffic moving across and, despite Interstate 40 pushing people on, averages suggest some will stop.

Mr Patel manages the Sunset Motel. He's been in Gallup eight years after a brief, unhappy period in Cleveland. I try my three phrases of Hindi which produces a laugh as he's from Gujarat and it's not his language. However, my token effort enlivens him to offer me a discount on the room as we share stories of Sanjay Dutt and the traffic in Bombay.

His brother preceded him to Cleveland and he moved

with hopes of a better education for his children, better exam results, better college, better life. He doesn't elaborate on how his plan has worked out.

In Bombay he was a businessman; import/export working five hours a day, mostly on administration. On arrival in America he packed boxes for twelve.

'When I first come I am sick with this country because no-one gives me a job. And when I get a job it is very poor job.'

A picture of Ganesh supplied by the Patel Brothers of Chicago as a promotional calendar gazed benevolently over his success at the administration desk.

'Once I was desperate but now I am settled it is no problem but you must keep the patience to go further and further and one day you will get your goal.'

On business, he suggests it could be better but is not unduly concerned. The town's fortunes dimmed when Interstate 40 by-passed it but that was ten years ago, before he arrived.

He jokes about the proximity of the railway line, suggesting the trains were nearer and more frequent in Bombay.

I ask him whether he plans to return to India. Again laughing, but then more serious, he suggests perhaps in a few more years when he's retired.

Rambling on to cricket and England he mentions a recent NBC report on Racism in London that appears to have given him the impression that Indian people are having a tough time in the UK.

'Not welcome anymore ?'

I assure him it's only a small minority. I can see in his eyes he's not sure but then neither am I. As I retire he offers a cup of tea in the morning, which turns out to be flavoured and very sweet. Indian tea.

As I'm leaving he takes an interest in the Honda and asks me the price.

'Very good cars these; I'll buy it when you come back through.'

He's disappointed to learn I won't be coming back. He asks to hear the engine fire once more before waving me away.

West of Gallup Interstate 40 forges through New Mexico into Arizona. This is the new road that has supplanted 66 as the national cross country highway. The old road still survives on its fringes, cutting in and out of old towns and the edge of cities stiff with manufactured nostalgia.

But it is not so easy to pull money off the interstate as it continues in moving isolation. On 66 cars only needed to slow down and stop, a moment's snap decision. With I-40 they must be motivated or persuaded to come off into town.

A mile short of the state line and I'm a successful catch of the hoarding promises as I drink coffee on the second floor of a forty-foot brick wigwam served by a surly waitress who is obviously not one of the friendly Navajos who are advertised to run and own this Indian Village Trading Post.

Ten miles up the Freeway, a series of hand-painted signs coloured in sun-bleached yellows and reds to match the tribal flag and omnipresent geology of the area began offering tax-free cigarettes, pottery at seventy-five per cent off and a real live buffalo at the Indian village. You are invited to bring a camera.

In a commercial world the Indians have begun to compete, aided in part by their own laws and a common culture educated on a celluloid history; they have a starting-point.

Here under the protection of sandstone cliffs which hang above a narrowing pass they have set up an ambush of gift shops, petrol stations and roadside cafés to catch the dollars that drive by.

The buffalo looked lonely, isolated in a small pen chewing a cud, but by then I had stopped.

Later in the day I pulled over again at the World's Biggest Truck Stop. It was crowded with people eating too much. The freeway can be one long sticky road of eating opportunities offering ferocious claims of cheap eating to the thin and unwary. The places change but the food remains the same.

From outside they are bright and hopeful underlined with a seeping smell of food that drifts down the freeway merging with the monoxide. Inside they are less upbeat, darker, the waitresses forcibly happy offering choices and specials.

Back in Tulsa Mally's diner on 11th street offers cheap food and is full on a Saturday morning as the waitresses skitter effortlessly around taking orders, refilling cups.

The locals stick to the tables, foreigners hug the bar hoping for more of the experience. A young Eastern couple sit opposite me and laugh easily. On the road together they are lured by the 66 sign. They study the menu for longer than is necessary, savouring the difference. Waiting for change. These are the faces that move with me, smiles that I know in faces that are strangers.

I return to the world's biggest. I watch as overweight people, wilting in the heat despite the air conditioning, refill another bowl from the all-you-can-eat salad bar.

M a r t h a

I'm pushing another ten dollars into the Honda. Another week has driven by on the road and I'm three hours short of Flagstaff. The Painted Desert is now a vague memory of colours; all splashes of red and a petrified forest laying flat and lifeless on eroding beds of mudstone. Real is back with a station forecourt and the injected count of numbers as the digits flash on.

The high blue New Mexico sky has fallen to the lower, more threatening clouds that are wandering over Arizona in a spate of Summer thunderstorms. A burst of wind twists over the forecourt scattering crisp-packets and till-receipts. There's a stain of smeared oil glistening with trapped water from an earlier storm but the clean concrete has been blown dry. I share the garage with three other travellers. Across the road is the obligatory Pizza Hut franchise.

'Excuse me, are you going west ?'

'Er yes,'

The accent is familiar but she's not American.

'Do you think I could take a lift with you ?'

'Er well I'm not sure,' I hesitate remembering the sign and the news report but she doesn't look threatening. Small, dark, with short cropped hair. A bright smile, big curling lips.

'How far are you going ?'

'I'm heading to Flagstaff, then perhaps the canyon.'

'Just to Flagstaff then ? Please ?'

This was not a difficult decision.

'Yeh okay.'

'Great.'

She beamed a smile as she threw a bright orange rucksack into the back of the Honda. I closed the fuel cap and looked upwards.

'Nice car.'

'Thanks.'

I slipped the car back on the Freeway. An eighteen-wheeler pulling cattle roared past.

'You going far ?'

'Maybe, Vegas perhaps.'

I asked the questions, she answered. Short clipped replies that she returned with a vague interest.

'Martha.'

'Australia.'

'Brisbane.'

'Three months.'

'Work.'

Okay, it was just a lift. I didn't need to get to know the passenger.

'Can I put a tape on ?'

'Yeh sure, in the dashboard.'

I began to relax as K.D. Lang twisted around the car. Martha put her feet up, slipped a pair of sunglasses on and began to sing quietly to herself. Flagstaff was suddenly just down the freeway.

The road passed through the fringes of a couple of towns. Just names on the freeway sliproad. Small towns, a name on the map. Whole lives echoing around streets and stores I never even pass through, just pass by. An unplanned stop could throw up something radical that could affect the whole journey or maybe just another fuel stop.

The road continued to climb onto the high Arizona plateau. Then the huddled peaks of the San Francisco mountains marked the town of Flagstaff where the pines had seeded down from the mountain to edge out onto the plain. To me Arizona should have been an arid desert and not a pine forest but the sign said Flagstaff; it was early evening and I needed a motel.

Martha was asleep, head lolling against the side of the rest, half-supported by the seatbelt. I touched her shoulder and she woke with a start, eyes wildly swirling in an attempt to focus and remember where she was. She looked frightened, suddenly almost vulnerable then her veil came down.

'I'm going to find a motel, you need somewhere to stay ?'

She looked out as a string of signs crowded the freeway.

'Flagstaff ?'

'Yeh, we're just coming in to the edge of town.' A series of restaurants eased by. The usual names. She absorbed it quickly.

'Fancy something to eat ?'

'I need a motel.'

'Nah eat first, there's hundreds of motels, you'll get a discount later.'

'Discount ?'

'Arrive late, get a discount.'

I looked to see if she was kidding but there was only a wide smile to confuse me. I pulled into an open empty car lot. The Alton Motel looked okay to me. Average diner, three fat men in check shirts, smell of coffee, tv tuned to the sports channel.

We walked in; I looked for the menu, Martha walked out.

I caught up with her in the car lot. 'What was wrong with that place ?'

'Didn't like it, this place will be fine.' She pointed across the lot to where a huge snorting but wooden bull was advertising Big Steaks at the Sizzler.

There was a queue at the door. They looked like RV drivers to me. Retired, white and grey. A sign at the door offered 40% discount to Seniors.

'This'll be good.'

I grabbed a tray from the pile. It was the first place I'd been without waitress service. Huge mounds of meat lay under the hot lights, beef steaks the size of bread boards with carefully-marked char grill lines. Thick slabs of chicken, white and bloated on steroids.

Martha ignored the meat and passed on to the salad bar. I remembered the stock feed lots and followed her.

An enormous plate of salad was only $3. Eat as much as you like, as many refills as you could stomach.

'You don't eat meat then ?'

'Disgusting dead flesh,' she winked as she popped a cherry tomato into her mouth.

'But what about all that dead flesh up there on the hot plate?'

'Can't change everything, can you?'

'Some people wouldn't eat in here out of principle.'

'Some people always take things too far. Anyhow, you'd starve.'

A waitress arrived to check if the salad was okay and did

we need anything else. Martha asked for a glass of iced water. I think the waitress guessed she wasn't going to get a tip.

The motels on the south side of town all looked a bit run down, so we drove through to the other side; they didn't improve but the the place was refreshingly small and actually had a center which looked like you could walk around.

'Try that one.'

The Ski Lodge offered doubles at $28 with air con and cable tv. The manager was another immigrant from Bombay, the same picture of Ganesh, the same smell of incense, the same promotional calendar from the Patel brothers of Chicago. He's from Dadar but doesn't know a Mr Patel from Gallup, formerly Cleveland. He looks at me impatiently and I shelve my Hindi greeting.

'Do you have any rooms?'

'Certainly, twenty-eight dollars including tax. Double room?'

I turn to Martha.

'Twenty-two for a twin?' She demands.

The manager looks as if he is about to fall off his stool.

'No discounts, twenty-eight is the price,' he replies tersely.

'Let's go.'

My mind goes blank as Martha heads for the door. I turn to apologise to the manager.

'Okay, twenty-two.'

I swallow hard and smile. Martha beams.

'Excellent.'

'How are you paying ?'

'Visa.'

I fill in the forms quickly. Martha watches the fish in a tank that bubbles delicately by the door. He's straining to ask a question but natural discretion frustrates him.

'Number thirty-two.' He hands me a round bulbous key.

'Thanks.'

We breeze out into the car park. The rooms are set back from the road in a long two-storey line. Each room has a marked car space. There's a view of the mountain behind and thirty-two is on the second storey.

'I couldn't believe you asked him for a discount.'

Martha fell onto the bed nearest the door. Her orange rucksack pushed up onto the pillow.

'Plenty of motels in town and it's the off season.'

'I thought he was going to have a stroke.'

She sighed deeply, 'I would have settled for twenty-five but he must have been out of practice, things usually cost more not less in this country.' She turned her head further into the pillow. 'God I'm tired, wake me if anything exciting happens.'

I try to relax on my bed, think of turning the television on low but dismiss the idea. Martha is face down, legs and arms apart, blue jeans rolled to her ankles, a dusty white t-shirt ruffled above her waist. I retrieve the book given to me by Jameson at Black Mesa. William Trogdon is still driving West. I scan five pages before I admit I'm not reading any of it. I check the bathroom, the toilet is clinically sanitised with a dust wrapper around the rim and a bar of free soap; the shower is lined with scarred blue tiles, the curtain bunched on the rail. I sit on the bed again and stare at the blank screen while picking my nails. I get up, flick through the directory of a hundred and one things to do in Flagstaff and forget them all instantly. It's getting dark; I try the view of the mountain, locking the door on the way out.

'Martha ?'
She moves but doesn't answer.
'Martha, fancy going out ?'
'Anything exciting happening ?'
'It's Flagstaff's centenary.'
'Wow.'
'There's a band on in a bar in town, supposed to be good.'
She turned over to face me. There was a red mark creased across her face where she had been lying on the edge of the pillow.
'Okay, give me five minutes for a shower.'

The soft fall of water seeped out of the bathroom as I played through another selection of channels. Their number had dwindled since Tulsa and all the news stations were carrying pieces on a war in Europe fifty years ago. Wizened old boys were stuffed into new uniforms and marching around a succession of cemeteries in France. Then interviews with the men back home in places like Kansas City and Denver, dwelling on sharp youthful memories of a blazing beach and a chance escape.

There's a story of a posthumous medal winner in the parachute regiment who spent two years training for the invasion, taught himself German and French, studied survival and sabotage techniques, memorised maps of the major routes through France. The invasion finally comes and he is standing in the doorway of the aircraft ready to lead his men in the jump. An anti-aircraft shell bursts in the door, tearing a hole in his chest. He staggers back before waving his men forward. They find him an hour later; dead and hanging from an apple tree.

A corporal from Washington recalls seeing a picture of German prisoners of war drinking coffee at a diner in one of the Southern States and knowing he wouldn't have been allowed the same privilege.

The stories continue.

I'm absorbed when the bathroom door is thrown open by Martha. She's wrapped in a grey towel that stops above her knees; hair is washed flat against her head. She walks around me, picks up her rucksack and disappears back behind the door. I breathe hard and flick the channel. Seconds later she's back in jeans and another white t-shirt.

'Where're we going then ?'
'The Boomtown Bar.'
'The Boomtown Bar ?'
'That's what the man said.'

We could have walked but we drove. I guess it becomes a habit. Leave your own personal safe haven as the last resort.

Flagstaff had hung out a few strings of bunting as a sop to its centenary. The radio invited everyone to a grand commemorative photograph in the Memorial Park on Friday afternoon; complimentary centenary flags for the kids.

The town slides down the hill from the Pinon-covered mountains bunching to a stop where the railway line rushes through. The trains screech a warning as they flow along the rails. Not many seem to stop and I can't find a station on the map.

The Boomtown Bar is in a rambling hotel on a corner lot sharing the ground floor with a coffee diner, a French

restaurant and the lobby. A billboard advertises Jake Myers
and his rhythm band for one night only.

The bar is easing up to half-full but we get a table ten
yards from a cramped stage in the corner of the room.
There's a guitar leaning against a stand and a lone keyboard
but no sign of Jake or his rhythm. An easy sway of
conversation hovers over the room. Big men swap money for
pitchers of clear, weak lager. There's still a few cowboy hats
but they're not as wide as further East.

Martha arrives with a pitcher of our own.

'Cheers,'

She smiles at me, a long sweet amused smile as if she's
still trying to work me out but is easy about the progress. I'm
thinking about her. Women alone always hold a fascination.
The confidence to be alone, needing no one. I consider a
plunge into further questions but recall the response from
the afternoon on the freeway. Perhaps it's easier just to sit
back and wait for the music.

'Thanks for the lift,'

'That's fine, I enjoyed the company.'

She stifles a giggle.

'I'm sorry I keep falling asleep, it's been a hard trip. But
I feel wide awake now, as long as the music's good.'

'Hey, Jake and the rhythm band are always good.'

She laughs this time, a sharp brief laugh, but then
allows herself a longer smile which forces me to a swill of my
lager.

'You been travelling long then ?'

'About three weeks.'

'From Chicago ?'

'No Tulsa.' She looked at me quizzically.

'How did you get to Tulsa ?'

'Flew.'

'You flew to Tulsa? Why ?'

'No reason, just a cheap flight.' I could tell she was intrigued and I was trying to sound as vague as possible.

'And now the canyon ?'

'Yeh, then who knows ?' We both knew I was lying but she seemed to be enjoying it.

There was a polite round of applause as Jake appeared from the shadows. He'd been drinking on the far corner of the bar and had obviously decided that the Boomtown wasn't going to boom any further. Another man rushed to join him from a table near the front where he had been sitting with a group of supporting friends.

Jake was a tall sallow character pushing forty from the front. There was a ragged look about him that suggested he had finally realised he wasn't going to be big after all and had settled on being ragged for a living. His companion on the keyboards was the rhythm band and Jake accompanied himself on the guitar.

He mumbled a brief introduction to the crowd who clapped appreciatively again before launching into a Guthrie/Dylan cover. He wasn't too bad; a rough Irish edge to his voice seemed to linger through the numbers. The crowd seemed to like him even if they were his friends.

Each song was preceded by a short dedication and forced banter between him and the threesome sitting around the front table. He didn't seem to want to address the other thirty listeners spaced around the bar. The keyboard player looked vacantly out into the spaces above the people.

The music rattled through while Martha and I drank the lager.

'Thank you, we'll take a break there but hold on 'cos

we'll be back.'

Another burst of applause, stronger this time, loosened by the alcohol, marked the interval.

'He's quite good.'

'Yeh, okay for an American.'

'Well how many Australians can sing like that ?'

'Loads, we're known as great singers.'

I couldn't gauge her humour. There was an undercurrent of sobriety in everything she said, as if daring me to test her commitment. But then the stream changed its depth and I was adrift again.

The bar filled further as the night deepened. More people leaning forward for a drink. Another round, more ease.

A friend of the rhythm's circled the tables with a box of cassettes.

'This is their third best-selling album.'

'Yeah ?'

'Best blues band in Arizona.'

'Sounded more country to me ?' commented Martha.

'Country blues.'

Martha giggled. The man turned to me.

'No thanks mate.'

He moved off to the next table.

'I thought you said you liked them ?'

'Yeah, didn't say I was going to buy one.'

'Could have been a bargain, third best-selling album ?'

'Well, I didn't think much of the first two.'

Martha looked at me with an air of surprise. I guess I can wisecrack too.

'Before Jake gets back up, what about another pitcher ?'

I squeeze myself to the bar. The second part has

dragged in a bigger crowd. People out on a Thursday evening in Flagstaff. Laughter and looks, slow drawn-out voices that seem to bulge as they elbow around the room. Bar girls spinning effortlessly between rounds and orders; money changing wallets, lager and the promise of light.

I watched Martha while I waited; eyes tuned to the distance beyond the stage. I wanted to know where she came from but hesitated to ask. The company was good; nice to sit in a crowded bar with a woman and watch the world trip by.

Jake had hollered into the second set by the time I had secured a full pitcher. Martha smiled in thanks as she accepted another glass. The music cut on; we smiled and drank, Jake mumbled more introductions, his friends and a few others clapped. A small group began dancing in a square of floor beneath the stage but most people were content to watch. I thought about asking Martha but I couldn't pick a song through the music, which had edged towards country.

'Thank you and goodnight.'

There was more applause and a one-song encore before Jake finally called it a night.

'Motel time.'

The sign still flashed insistently for twenty-eight dollars including tax but it had failed to pull in any more cars. A smattering of lights back lit the few occupied rooms on the second storey.

We climbed to thirty-two without talking. Martha didn't seem to be into conversation but she wasn't difficult to be around. The room welcomed with a sterile anonymity; grey whites and washed out covers. The beds were divided by a table supporting a phone, everything faced the far wall and the television.

'Fancy a coffee?'

'No thanks, I'll be peeing all night.'

She collapsed onto the bed.

'Martha ?'

'Yeh ?'

I guess she knew I was going to make an offer.

'Tomorrow, if you haven't got any other plans, I'm going up to the north rim of the canyon, if you fancy the slow way to Vegas for a couple of days ?'

'You sure you can cope with me ?'

She flicked a question across her eyebrows. A ripple of nerves drifted down my spine.

'Yeh, I think so.'

'The canyon sounds good to me.' She turned and pushed the light by the bed. A faint glow from the car-lot security lights filtered through the shutters as I listened to Martha undress and slip into the single bed.

I lay awake for a long time on top of the covers staring at the ceiling and listening while her breathing softened slower into sleep.

We hauled out of the Ski Lodge late. Martha wasn't keen on an early start. A bed was for lying in, motels for using. I was in no rush to go anywhere and she knew it. The road had merged from the open grasslands of Oklahoma, through the high blue ridge of the Sangre de Cristo mountains to the drier baked desert west of Gallup. It was becoming a succession of motels and diners all serving the moving. I had been in a rush to get across, get it over with. Now there was Martha; slow, easy and enjoying the ride. I was going to Vegas by the long route.

I fought off a maid who muttered Hindi beneath her breath through the chained door.

'We've got to check out by eleven.'

Martha had moved from the bed to the bath.

'They've got plenty of rooms.'

'The maid wants to get in.'

'Maid ?'

I resorted to the tv again and was absorbed into a discussion on female wrestlers. Muscled women with incredible hairstyles talked confidently about the sporting aesthetics of wrestling in G-strings and bikini tops.

Centenary day in Flagstaff was ticking towards midday. Martha was still in the bathroom.

'Hey, if you're not out of there soon I'm going.' The talk show had finished.

'No you're not.'

I turned over.

We drove back through town to pick up Highway 89. The park in the center was crowded with people surrounding a fireman's crane.

'It's the centenary photograph.'

'What ?'

'The photograph, they invited us yesterday on the radio. C'mon let's be part of history.'

I looked to see if she was serious and as far as I could tell she was.

The host radio station was broadcasting from an immodest yellow van parked on the steps of the town's library which served as a bookend to the park with a terrace and a couple of statues.

A thick rope of wires led from the van to a trestle table where two men held a conversation between themselves and whoever was turned into KYZ 100. They were big, overfed men who seemed to be enjoying the release from a cramped studio and the strain of constantly imagining an audience. The audience here was real and stretched out onto the grass slopes of the park or huddled under the cherry trees. No one in the audience seemed to be listening to them but they kept at it anyway; talking too loud into speakers and throwing their arms around to emphasise the size of their insults which were mostly directed at Hillary and Bill as if they were on first name Christmas card terms with Hillary and Bill. Old friends from Little Rock.

'Now, Bill he's just plain stupid, just stupid.'

The insults were gross and, as is the need of insults, insulting, but then this wasn't an intelligent debate.

The crowd continued to ignore them, concentrating instead on the attempts of the fire brigade to persuade the Centenary photographer that he was safe in the lift. He didn't seem to be keen but this was an important assignment. The big picture had been advertised for three. There was another twenty minutes; more people appeared, walking in from the town eager to get a slice of history.

Martha drifted off and reappeared holding two ice-cream cones.

'What flavour do you want?' She pushed them towards

me. They looked remarkably alike, glowing the same red colour.

'What's the choice ?'

'Strawberry or strawberry.'

I took one of the cones.

'My favourite's strawberry and this way even if I give you the choice I still get the strawberry.'

I took a bite of the coloured cone.

'When's the picture ?'

'Another twenty minutes.'

She scanned the people in the swelling crowd. Families. Middle class America.

'They're kind of white.'

'Yeh, I see what you mean.'

The guy in the fireman's tower was waving frantically for the crowd to squeeze together so he could get all of them in the shot. A few obliged but not many. Eventually a fireman climbed the tower with a loud hailer and the crowd obediently began to drift closer in. People smiled at strangers, cracked uncomfortable jokes or just looked up.

Ten minutes later we were still standing together. The man appeared to be a perfectionist. The radio station played 'The Battle Hymn of the Republic' on the turn of the hour, the crowd cheered, then edged gratefully apart from their short intimacy.

'We're in the history books.' Martha was obviously pleased with the afternoon.

'Hey look at that guy.' She pointed to a throw of shade under one of the cherry-trees where a flock of children had surrounded a man wearing a black top hat. He was also wearing a long-tailed coat, a deep red waistcoat, pinstriped trousers and a Boa Constrictor around his neck. I guessed the attraction was the snake but why the hat and the tails?

Martha walked over for a closer look. I was distracted by a man from National Public Radio interviewing a couple of kids. He asked short, obvious questions and then waited as the kids thought out serious, considered answers.

'I'm glad Flagstaff was founded. I don't want to move away. I was born on Cherry Street.'

'You were born in the hospital,' piped his younger sister.

'I was born in the hospital but I lived on Cherry Street.'

The interviewer prompted him further.

'I like Flagstaff because there's mountains to hike on and trees and canyons and there's a whole lot of bears in Oak Creek Canyon.'

'What's one thing you can say about Flagstaff?' The interviewer asked the boy's sister.

'Flagstaff's cool.'

The crowd had trickled away, back to the tree-filled avenues that surrounded the town. I watched a few stragglers talking on the green.

'He says I can take his photograph.' Martha was excited; her lips creased wide across her face.

'The snake ?'

'Sure the snake, what else ?' She pushed a camera at me. 'Just aim and press, it focuses itself.'

I followed her back to the cherry tree where the top-hatted gentleman smiled sweetly at me as he draped the doped snake around her neck. I smiled quickly back. Martha twirled once, then set herself for the picture. The snake clung on. I pressed.

'Thank you.'

'It was my pleasure, miss.' He winked and passed her a card, then tipped his hat gently.

I nodded my head away, indicating we needed to go.

'Thank you again, you're sweet.'

She waved back as we headed for the Honda.

'What was on his card?'

She opened the palm of her hand.

'J.S. Mecurio. Magician.'

'Never.'

'What else do you think he was with a top hat and a snake?'

I thought about that one for a while.

Highway 89 curled around the San Francisco mountains before heading north-west on a long, slow glide into the canyon. The desert reappeared again as the trees lost out to the dry winds of the plateau. I settled into the drive but we needed gas before entering the canyon.

Martha looked happy; she smiled out at the land, then at me, then the land. I didn't mind sharing her smiles with the land.

The five o'clock news on the radio carried a story of a Navajo embezzling funds from the tribe's casino business. He was to be thrown out of the tribe for five years and banned from standing for election for another fifteen. Another item followed: a senior Democratic senator trying to fight his way out of a corruption charge in which he was accused of fiddling his mail allowance for what he seemed to consider was a trivial amount. He wasn't about to go quickly or quietly and the party was worried about the health bill, the path of which he was supposed to be leading through Congress before he posted a few letters too many.

We pass a State of Arizona Dangerous Plant control post. White and blue concrete; boarded-up windows. Peeling paint from the sign which persists in requesting destruction of all foreign vegetable matter long after the dangerous plants had passed through.

I take a few pictures and a wagon passes on the highway pulled by two mules. A man with skin the colour of hazelnuts hunches forward over the reins concentrating on the steady line of highway back up the mountain towards Flagstaff. Cars and trailers fly past him in bursts but his face remains impassively set on the road. The mules, blinkered and inured to the rush, pull the covered wagon, festooned with collected giveaways, slowly on.

I wave but the man remains hunched forward. Martha has been lulled into sleep.

I look at the sign, then the paint, then the wagon. All passing time.

Further on an Exxon garage ambushes the highway from a rocky mound above the desert. Bold red letters emphasize the Exxon and I remember the Valdez running aground. Its progress has been stuttering through the Summer news reports in *U.S.A Today* as the case builds momentum in the civil courts. Its hulk a profitable wreck for the lawyers. The company looks as if it is going to hit a reef of heavy fines. Thousands of Innuit claiming disruption of livelihood. The company defends itself with bland apologies and an expensive legal team.

But with the News the reality always intrudes.

'I'll get this one.'

I accept the offer as Martha heads for the cash desk.

'Twenty dollars ?' she shouts back.

'Twenty dollars and a coke.'

I wait for the amount to be programmed into the computer before I can draw some gas. I guess they got fed up with driveaways. To get something free from an American gas station you now need to hold it up.

I once hitched a lift with two bikers in a Triumph 2000 outside Exeter. They were heading for Newquay but were short of petrol.

'We can take you to the next garage .'

I was nervous but needed the lift.

We drove deep into Devon along the A30 before they found one that they obviously liked. Wide open forecourt, left hand side of the road. The driver turned to me as he pulled the car alongside the pump.

'This is it kid, I'm afraid.'

'Yeh no problem, thanks for the lift anyway.' I was glad to get out. Their conversation of a drunken night in Derby and who might have got glassed with the jagged edge of a Newkie Brown bottle had been making me uneasy.

'Do you mind getting us a can and chocolate from the shop?' He flicked me a fifty pence piece.

'Yeh sure, anything in particular.'

'Nah, whatever.'

His friend in the front, who until now had been referred to as Spike, as in "Spike shut the fuck up" stifled a giggle.

I smiled, delivered my fond but eager farewells and headed for the shop.

I was third in the queue. I decided the driver was a Mars man. The till rang efficiently as I watched him pump the car with petrol. He slowly replaced the nozzle, screwed his petrol cap in place. Sat back into the car and drove the Triumph straight out of the garage back onto the A30.

I was still watching him go when the cashier asked me for fifteen quid.

But in the UK I guess they were a minority.

'You going up the highway ?'

I turn to face a black-haired man staring hopefully and pointing in the direction of Flagstaff. He's wearing a pale blue shirt stained with oil and a lighter colour my accelerating imagination suggests is blood.

'No sorry, I'm heading for the canyon.'

His smile fades a bit but not too much.

'Just I needed a lift, come off my bike, two miles across the reservation and the boys don't know where I'm at.'

'Are you alright ?'

'Yeh, just bounced up a bit, just need a lift.'

'Sorry, wrong direction, but I've got some bandages.'

'No, it's just shallow. Just the boys don't know where I am. They went ahead without me, we were going for a couple of beers twenty-eight miles that way and I'm kinda running behind. Now it's all shot.'

'Sorry.'

'Aw it doesn't matter, anyway where you from ? Sounds

a strange accent, somewhere east ?'

'Wales.'

'Long swim ?'

'Yeah.'

'And you speak English.'

'Usually.'

'Everyone speaks English now, even the Navajos.'

'You Navajo?'

'Sure, do I look like anything else ?'

I shrugged my shoulders.

'Live out on the reservation,' he pointed out across the desert.

'Doesn't look like there's much out there ?'

'There's nothing out there but there's a whole lot of people living out there, whole lot of people.'

'What do they do out there ?'

'Oh, we live, get by, you know. Keep some sheep, fix a few cars. That's where I've been now.'

'Fixing cars ?'

'Nah, shearing. There's no electricity out there, been out a week now, long way out there.'

He was concerned about the language fading away and told me a story about how Navajo wireless operators in WWII had been used to communicate field orders fooling the Germans into thinking they were speaking in code.

'We've got our own radio station now and the elders try to get everyone to speak Navajo on the reservation. You can speak English everywhere, any damn fool will learn that language. I couldn't speak any before I went to school and listen to me now.' He smiled a big wry smile. 'You speak Welsh ?'

'Bits.'

'Should speak you're own language man, you'll lose yourself.'

Martha returned with two cans of coke. She beamed a smile to the man. He stretched his own a little further.

'You okay ?'

'Sure, just come off my bike, bounced up a bit.'

'You sure ?'

'Yeh.'

'Have a drink.' She passed him one of the coke cans.

'Thanks, miss.' He pulled open the top and poured half the can straight down his throat. 'Getting a bit dry, hot work falling off bikes.' The man grinned further before topping off the can. 'Well, thank you, I'd better get my thumb out on the highway if I'm going to make town.'

'Sorry we couldn't help you.'

'No problem, you just enjoy the canyon.'

The man wandered off across the forecourt. The wind pulled a shower of dust off the desert, pushing it across the concrete out onto the highway.

'Good place to meet people.'

'Where ?'

'Forecourts.'

'Yeh, not bad.'

Martha passed me the coke, slid her sunglasses over her nose and reclined into the seat.

Nice day in the desert.

Shadows in the grass

The land seems too big for the people who make their lives out of it. The unease lingers at the edge of towns, signs for diners or cigarettes forty feet high in futile attempts to compensate for the vastness of a continent which narrows a history to a few shallow decades.

The older immigrants drive on, unsure of their forgotten history, unaware of the whispers of an earlier people who were at ease with the rhythms of the land but are now only shadows, fleeting as the winds that course the grass.

⁊**ல**

The road dipped over the edge of the plateau and followed a long dry valley north. The land was parched; white and red boulders; sand patches and pebble beds. Low, fierce shrubs crouched tight against the wind and the sun. A ghost river flowed at the base of the valley; meanders, shallows and waterfalls marked its ephemeral path running north, chipping at the sandstone bedrock that jutted upwards in bursts of red obstinacy.

A spine of jagged mountains followed the progress of the valley. Thick bands of strata flowing in low waves marked out by the quick change of colours from white to red and back to white again as they rode to the crest. Each bed a hundred thousand years as a shallow sea dried to desert and flooded back to sea again.

As the valley deepened, small wooden stalls began ambushing the highway from the safety of gravel lay-bys. Old women and young girls sat behind, selling painted bowls, brightly-coloured bangles and stoned rings for a few dollars apiece. Hanging from the wooden crosswork were framed nets that fluttered in the finest breeze. A small sign advertised the acceptance of five major credit cards.

I pointed at one of the funnel-shaped nets.

'Five dollars.'

The woman smiled, a tired dust-spoiled smile expecting me to know what they were.

Martha did.

'They catch your dreams, protect you from nightmares.'

'Yeh ?'

I fumbled in my jeans for five dollars.

'What you want one for ?'

'I don't know, they look okay.'

'You dream too much already.' She winked at me.

'How would you know ?'

'I can tell.'

She waited for a response but I just let go of the dollars in my pocket. The woman behind the stall scowled at her.

We moved on to the next stall.

'Look, buy me one of these.' She pointed at a silver twisting snake strung on a leather cord. The girl behind sat up to get a better view of us. She was young, fat and looked very bored.

'Eight dollars.'

Martha placed the snake around her neck and smiled at me. I pushed my hand back into my jeans.

'Thanks.' She kissed me on the cheek; then twirled, the snake pulling out from her body. I gave the girl ten dollars and forgot about the change.

As we moved away from the stall the first sheet of a moving thunderstorm brushed across the gravel sending the stall-holders rushing for rolls of clear plastic which they secured over their wares. We dived into the Honda as the storm thickened and a first flash of lightning was followed quickly by a crack of thunder. Thick spots of rain rapped on the roof and streamed down the windscreen, tracing channels in red dust that had blown in from the desert.

Martha brushed the rain from her face up into her hair.

'I love the rain, it reminds me of Australia.'

'Rain ?'

She blew more water from her top lip.

'Yeah, I worked a season at Yulara and I didn't see rain for eleven months; everything had died away; the plants shrivelled close to the ground as if they had given up hope. Even the flies seemed to have less time for you in the heat. Then just after Christmas these huge clouds began appearing from the south.' She paused to confirm that I was listening. 'Really enormous clouds with huge thunderheads on them spilling up into the blackness as if they were never going to come down, then we could see showers, huge falls of water in the distance and then it rained, rained like like I'd never seen it before, floods of water like the whole ocean had decided to come back and reclaim the center of the desert. Floods everywhere, huge torrents of water in wadis that had been dry for years. All the roads were out; a party of Japanese had to be airlifted out because the roads were flooded. Imagine that, being marooned by floods in the center of Australia.'

She paused briefly in the rush of the memory.

'Then after the rain had eased a bit, only a couple of days later, the whole place erupted in new shoots and flowers as if they were all in a big rush to be out of the ground after waiting so long in a scramble for life. There were even pools at the base of the Rock, just hollows in the stone that had been dry and dead for years and they were full of frogs and water beetles all madly shagging each other. And birds, hawks and finches just appeared, flocks of them to gorge on the life. All because of the rain.'

She looked at me nervously. Suddenly, sort of embarrassed by her long burst of enthusiasm. A monologue which seemed huge by her standards.

'That's why I like the rain.'

She pushed her sunglasses back up her nose from where they kept sliding, flicked a loose lock of hair away from her face and looked straight ahead.

The light was fading quickly as we crossed the canyon at its northern mouth. A steel bridge, the only one across the gorge, held the road 300 feet above the Colorado river which shivered in the darkness below.

A sign pulled us left to a State park ten miles off the highway. The thunderstorm had swollen to cover the whole sky as the twisting road cut around boulders the size of houses that had been cast off from the cliffs above.

The state park was almost empty; too small for the RVers who needed a hook-up and at least a hot tub if not a swimming pool. It was run on more austere lines, with only a toilet block and no showers. The camp host reckoned it kept people moving through. There was an eight-day limit on a site. A few tents; hiking tents clawed a hold on the gravel at the far end, a circle of camper vans closer to the river.

I peered out through the rain. The windscreen wipers flicked efficiently across and back for the first time since Tulsa.

The host appeared reluctant to come out of his camper. I wound down the window.

'Anywhere ?'

'Yeh, sure son, pay in the morning,' he shouted from his open door before retreating into the dry.

I could see the flicker of the tv and the pulse of a baseball game through the net curtains.

'You any good at putting tents up ?'

Martha looked at me. 'In the rain ?'

'I thought you liked the rain ?'

'Yeh, I just don't like putting tents up in it.'

'It's more fun in the rain.'

'Why ?'

'Sense of excitement. Don't get that in the dry.'

'Balls mate.'

'C'mon.'

A burst of hail rattled over the roof.

'What about sleeping in the car ?'

'Too small.'

'She'll be fine.'

'Too small.'

She hunched her head into her shoulders as she peered out.

'Shit.'

I pulled the car to the far side of the site where a wrought iron sun shelter shivered in the rain. The camp rose on a hill above the canyon. A long bolder-strewn slope tapered into willows and shrub on the edge of the river. The far bank rose into a high, stepped cliff coloured by horizontal beds of sandstone. A deeper red of an earlier desert. The sky was grey shading to black where the thunder thickened in the darkness. Sharp forks of lightning flashed further up the canyon.

'Right ?'

Martha looked straight ahead. Not wanting to answer.

I dipped the window again to view our pitch. A blast of warm desert air engulfed the car; the scents were so much stronger in the rain. Thick redolent odours of dried shrubs and flowers carried by the wind.

The rain seemed to be easing but the thunderstorm was trapped in the canyon. It spat petulant sparks of lightning, frustrated by the sharp canyon sides and a shelf of cold air holding it down. The heavy claps echoed off the walls; howling. The canyon chuckled with echo, happy with its catch.

'This okay ?'

'Give it five.'

We waited for five minutes. I counted the turn of the revolving clock tucked into the red dashboard of the Honda. As it turned to seven thirty-nine, I opened the door.

'It's easing.'

'Yeh sure.'

I love putting tents up in the rain. Good memories.

The tent billowed out as I struggled with the flysheet, which was waving furiously in the wind. I'd jammed the third peg into the ground when Martha appeared.

'Give me some pegs.'

The rain seemed to ease and we secured the tent on the

second attempt. It looked a bit lopsided, lurching to one side, but I reckoned it would hold until the morning. Once we were in it.

I threw a sleeping bag in from the boot of the car. Then a couple of towels. When I squeezed through the entrance Martha was sitting up with her knees under her chin and her arms clasped around her legs.

'Do you want a towel ?'

She seemed far away; her eyes glazed; mind at some other moment. I pushed the towel towards her. She took it without changing her expression.

I ruffled the towel through my hair. Martha still looked forward. I tried to ignore her.

'I haven't got a sleeping bag.'

'Oh.'

She smiled at me bleakly.

'I've got a blanket in the car; you have this one.'

'Thanks.'

I headed back out to the car. When I returned Martha was already in the bag. Her head resting on her rolled jeans.

'Nice tent.'

'Thanks.'

Darkness had slipped in over the canyon rim as the world closed to the dimensions of a two-person tent. The rain tapped on the coated nylon; whispering. I waited as its insistent voice pushed me into sleep.

Tumbleweed

I picked the Tumbleweed up in Cimarron County. It had been caught in the rusting wires of a steer fence that fringed the road. The fence aping a gill net that trapped shoals of wandering Tumbleweeds as they traversed the flat tablelands.

I hung it in the back of the Honda from the suit hook. It seemed happy, content to be on the move again and whirred with a faint whisper as it conspired with the wind when I wound the window down.

It was a great source of conversation. People stopped me in car parks of supermarkets to ask where I got it from. The policeman who checked my license in Albuquerque reckoned he knew where I could get a whole bunch more of them, real cheap. I had to get a ticket for it when I drove into the Petrified Forest, just in case the warden on the other gate suspected I'd rustled it from the park. The Tumbleweed was in demand.

I'd recognized the Tumbleweed from a thousand Saturday-night Westerns when two-horse towns with a weak or crooked sheriff brought in a hired gun to shoot up the outlaws ensconced on a ranch out on the range. The outlaws were usually brothers with a wizened old patriarch running the show while the hired gun was a man without a past or a past filled with rumours. The tumbleweed appeared in the first few scenes to imply dereliction or just before the end to herald a showdown. But it was always there as a hard-edged immigrant extra hijacking its way into American world culture.

It first arrived on a boat somewhere in the 1850s as part

of a mass flight from feudal poverty in Eastern Europe but was quick to lose its identity as it swarmed over the flat prairies and desert that stretched across the open Western States.

It struggled for a century, rootless, without a history, always blowing through to the next town in search of a future while trying to forget the past. By the end of the 'thirties it was firmly entrenched, its many faces and languages merged under a uniform white English-speaking front of striving success. The Tumbleweed was ready for an assault on world domination that would prove irresistible.

The World believed, bought and wanted more.

The many faces are still there, easily visible with strong voices, but abroad it is only the distilled, refined and polished image that people want. Concentrated packaged forms of successful youth or successful middle age or successful pensioners.

I sold the car in San Francisco, put the Tumbleweed in a box, marked it as a hat and posted it home Sea Mail.

Paria Beach

The morning was high and bright. The sun pulling us from the tent before Seven. Martha seemed eager to get out. High wisps of cirrus were the only smudges on a clear blue sky. The valley looked washed; sparkling in the sunshine. The gravel was drying quickly; small channels in the dust were the only reminder of the evening's heavy rain.

'What a day.'

'I love this country, it's so full of change.'

We walked slowly down to the base of the canyon chewing three-day-old bagels and soft cheese. A few other campers were already out; brisk good mornings exchanged, brightened by the height of the sky.

The road ended in a loop a hundred metres from the river. A wood of willow marking the bank where the trees could rely on the constancy of the flow in a dry desert.

A sandy path followed signs to Paria Beach. One more ridge before the rush of noise and light flooded up from the river where it thudded into the far sandstone bank. It was narrow; much narrower than I expected but flowing brutally fast with shining, clear water that rose in clouds of condensation where the rapids were quickest. Further down the flow calmed and deepened, curving huge eddies along the near side that brushed up on a shallow beach of white sand.

'Wow, a real beach.'

I looked along the length of sand to where it stopped half a mile along the river in a rising terrace of cliff and boulders. Further south the walls of the canyon narrowed again, marking the true start of its descent into the bedrock.

'Fancy a day on the beach ?'

'I thought you wanted to keep moving ?'

'It's a day on the beach.' It looked like a good place to ease off and the water needed a swimmer.

'Yeh, always fancy a day on the beach.'

'Great.'

Two fishermen cast spinners out in turning water just below the rapids. Pulling them back slowly; waiting.

A Welsh Wedding

The sun had settled above the canyon when we returned to the beach; temperature rising quickly. We walked half way along where a group of willows dripped down from the bank, throwing a thin shade across the fine sand. A lizard scuttled up the slope from where it had been sucking warmth on a flat stone. Cicadas whirred listlessly in the scrub beyond the bank.

Martha stretched a towel out on the sand and lay back, waiting for the sun to warm her. A washed-out green swimmer's suit rippling across her body. I hadn't seen this much of her before.

I walked to the edge of the river, tucking my toes under the sand where the water joined the shore. I needed a swim.

'Coming for a dip ?'

'Nah not yet.'

I waded out a few yards. The water was so cold it carved a deep heavy pain into my legs.

'Shit.'

Martha raised herself up on her elbows.

'What's the matter ?'

'It's freezing.'

'Wimp,' she chided, laughing at my predicament.

It was ninety degrees, it was Arizona, it was a desert. The water was as cold as anything I'd ever swum in.

I waded out a few more yards as I began to lose feeling in my legs.

'Go on.'

I looked back at Martha. She was enjoying it. The water

swirled up higher as I waded out. The next couple of inches were going to be painful. I could edge out, gradually getting used to it, but I don't think I could have become inured to water that cold; or I could plunge.

I closed my eyes as I dived. A sharp rush of shock engulfed my body. I broke the surface in a scream of water and air, frantically trying to swim. Five or six strokes out and I gave up; spinning in the current I turned back and scrambled back up the sand bank.

'It's too cold.'

She laughed at me as I shivered in water up to my knees. I warmed quickly in the dry hot air but I didn't fancy another go, not yet.

'That's it ?'

'Yeh, for now.'

I paddled back to the shore and Martha lay back. The interest gone.

'Thought you were a real man.'

The morning drifted on in the sun. The fishermen continued casting down the rapids. A couple of rafts flooded past on a fourteen-day trip down the river.

The tours were organized from a base at Lee's Ferry a mile or so upstream. After Pariah beach the only way out for two weeks was a walk up to the rim. The rafts were huge, carrying eight or ten people a-piece and loaded with supplies for the trip. Tents, food and barrels of cooking fuel all lashed on by roped netting. The crews waved cheerfully as they passed. I could see the excitement on their faces. Big adventure.

I read more of Moon while Martha snoozed. Nice easy day on the river.

Towards one I worked out the time difference between

Paria Beach and Porthcawl, reckoning it was well into evening on the Welsh coast.

'Fancy a wedding toast ?'

Martha didn't reply but I knew she was awake. I repeated the offer.

'I know what you said, I was just trying to work it out.'

I picked out two bottles of beer the river had been cooling at the edge of the water. Big heavy bottles with clear, light American lager.

'Chilled.'

Martha pushed herself up onto her elbows.

'The man has style, although it could have been champagne,' she added with a generous smile.

I flicked the two metal caps over with a bottle opener and passed Martha one of the beers.

'No glasses, I'm afraid.'

She grasped the bottle and raised it to her lips.

'Hang on, I haven't proposed the toast yet.'

'Yeh I forgot.'

'To John and Mair.'

'To John and Moira.'

'No, Mair.'

'That's what I said, Moira.'

'Mairre.'

'Mairre.'

'That'll do.'

'To John and Mairre.'

'Oh, and Sara.'

'Sara ?'

'Their daughter.'

'Right.'

We both drank a gulp of the beer. I winced at the taste

but it was cold.

'I take it they're getting married today ?'

'They should be married by now but I guess you wouldn't have appreciated it at four this morning.'

She swallowed another gulp of lager.

'It's good, it reminds me of Queensland.'

'Yeh.'

Martha looked at me suspiciously but I just smiled.

'And there's food ?'

I pulled out the remainder of the bagels and cheese while we toasted a wedding in Wales.

Towards two she finished the bottle, smiled, then kissed me once before folding up on my chest, pulling small rises out of brown skin with the curling hairs until she fell asleep.

Hopi

I woke to the stare of a chubby little girl who was casting a deeper shade over us than the willows.

'Will you play with us ?'

I focused lazily. The girl smiled down; big eyes magnified by a pair of moon spectacles, dark hair, pink black-spotted bathing costume. I smiled back and gently shook Martha awake.

'Will you play with us ?' She repeated her request as another small girl arrived to stare down at us. She was smaller and thinner, without the glasses.

'This is my sister, Marsha.' The sister smiled obediently, then added, 'Will you play with us ?'

Martha turned around and stared at them. 'Ambush,' she moaned, rolling off onto the sand to get a better look.

'Hello.'

'Hello,' they chorused.

'What's your names again ?'

'I'm Amy and this is...'

'Marsha.' Her sister piped, desperate to speak for herself.

'Her name's Marsha.'

'I'm Martha. That's so close to your name, let me see, it's almost the same lettering.'

'I can spell my name.' Marsha drew her name in the sand. Her big sister looked a little put out by the immediate connection but she was being patient.

'See here's my name, just the same except for the S which is a T.'

The little girl beamed.

'Can you play with us now ?'

'Well I'm not sure, where's your mother ?'

'Over there.' They pointed eagerly at a woman sitting forty yards along the beach. She waved nicely back.

'I guess she thinks it's alright.'

'Yes, we asked her.'

'Oh.'

'What you want to do then ?'

'Carry us to the island.' They pointed out into to the shallows where the sandbank I had dived from shimmered just beneath the surface. Martha turned to me.

'Your turn.'

'Thanks.' I pushed myself up from the sand.

'I'm first.' Amy raised her hand.

She was a lot heavier than she looked as she clambered

onto my back. I waded out to the sandbar, placed her down in the knee-deep water, then carried her back.

When we reached the bank her mother had moved up the beach to talk with us. She was a big, beautiful woman with a toddler in one arm and a young boy a little younger than Amy but older than Marsha clinging to her leg.

'I see you're the ferry service.'

Martha laughed. Marsha had lost interest in the sand bar.

'I'm Ruth and this is my little tribe, we're Hopi.' They were on a day out to the river. Father was keen to use his fishing license for the new season and the children had been promised a swim but the water was too cold. They lolled around on the edge of the sand getting bored and wishing they had been taken shopping instead. Memorial Day was dragging by.

'He's down the bank away.' She pointed to a figure casting from the boulders at the far end of the beach. 'I'm giving him another twenty minutes, then it's the supermarket.'

She was a nice, friendly woman who wanted to know where we were from, what we were doing and didn't even pretend to be shocked that we weren't married, although she was a Mormon by religion.

'A lot of Hopi are Mormon now.'

We swapped addresses and she invited us back to her home in Page for fried bread and tea. We promised perhaps later in the week, knowing we were heading the other direction.

'Well, if you're passing.'

The children were shy with their mother talking. Playing small games between themselves. Hoping to attract our attention.

'His time's up, we'll be going or the shops will be shut, Memorial Day an' all.'

They moved off happily towards the rapids and the car park. The fisherman was bound to follow as they had his tackle box.

A few minutes later a thin wiry man smiled as he loped past us on the trail.

Driftwood

We lazed through the warm afternoon, opening another bottle of beer, telling each other stories as we kissed. Our skin sliding and sticking as the sweat trickled out in the heat. The river flowed on twisting after the first quick rapid to lazy, languorous eddies, curling over the sand bar that still glistened in the sun. Towards evening we swam to wash the thick scents of the afternoon away.

As we dressed, a beaver pushed out from a driftwood dam, holding its nose high until, sensing us, it dived, leaving only a shimmer of ripples. We didn't see it again.

Lee's Ferry

At dusk we walked up to a homestead set back from an old ferry crossing of the Colorado. A barred gate had 'Lonely Dell Ranch' cut into grey weathered timber, marking the mouth of a tributary canyon. The floor of the canyon opened out on to a terrace of finer soil that had been cultivated into a scatter of fields. Tired old plum trees and a brace of shackled barns fringed a deserted longhouse.

The place was thick with ghosts. Cultivated ghosts. The darkest still framed in old pictures and words from a century ago. The ranch had been named by one of the wives of John Doyle Lee who history has claimed as the first white settler in the area. He arrived at the canyon with two wives and a growing band of children to operate a ferry service sponsored by the Mormon Church in 1871. The Church needed a route south for its settlers, who were heeding a call and moving into Arizona. He was a man with a bloody past. He had been on the run from a murder charge for fourteen years through his involvement with the Mountain Meadows Massacre in 1857.

Lee had led a band of Mormons intent on frightening non-church followers from settling in Utah. Dressed as Navajos, they attacked and massacred a settler's wagon caravan of over a hundred people on their way to San Francisco. The simple subterfuge was soon discovered and Lee was on the run. To some in the Church, Lee remained a hero even after he faced a firing squad at the end of a harsh Utah Winter in 1877. The Mormons would fight to keep the independence and seclusion they had wrested from the desert. Lee kept ahead of the guns for twenty years, the ferry at the mouth of Paria canyon remote enough to hide him, although it would soon carry his name.

A man named Johnson replaced Lee. He lasted another fifteen, abandoning the ranch soon after he lost four children within four months when a passing wagon train gave away clothes rank with diphtheria. The headstones crowd together in an overgrown cemetery on the ranch road.

After Johnson the ranch and the area attracted dreamers and prospectors fired on hopes of gold-mining, ranching and even tourists. The canyon seems to have broken them all. The ribs of a paddle steamer, the Charles H. Spencer, lies in the river after being dragged overland from San Francisco. The steamer, financed by East Coast investors was to haul coal from a shaft 28 miles downstream to power a speculative gold-mining operation. It was abandoned after only five journeys. Its owner of the same name went the same way as his dreams of a quick fortune. Leo and Hazel Weaver tried and failed with a dude ranch in the 'thirties. Stories drifted with the sand or were blown away by the wind.

The sun had fallen early behind the canyon cliffs, leaving a grey light which flooded the homestead, sketching shadows that played with my sight. A jackrabbit flicked off the path, rises of dust hanging in the air long after it had merged with the scrub.

Martha

What was she? A dream.

All those people you smile at and they smile back and ask why? Why not you and I? Do we dare ? How many other lives can you easily slip across to without a glance? How many different roads when we only try one and only once?

Evening

The tent was warmer that night. We used the sleeping bag as a mattress and shared the blanket. It was good to feel the warm weight of a woman curled around me. The easy thick slide of silent, strange, unknown sex. Smiles and short soft noises at night that promise a thousand possibilities.

I waited a long time before a heavy sleep carried me into the morning.

Sunday we headed for the North Rim. Memorial Day weekend was halfway gone and the roads still looked empty. A car ten minutes away along the highway flashing silver in the sun. A pair of cyclists, head down pushing against the low wind, trying to make the miles before the sun climbed too high.

Martha made me stop for a photograph. A sandstone boulder the size of a truck perched on a pedestal of mudstone. The mudstone had been winnowed away by the wind and the rain but remained as a pillar where it was sheltered by the hard sandstone boulder. It looked like a fantastic rock mushroom.

Martha stood under it, pretending to hold it up. Big lips, smiling teeth, t-shirt and shorts, barefeet. She looked goofy.

'Thanks.'

'Holiday snap ?'

'Prize for the dumbest pic when I get back to Brisbane.'

'Who with ?'

'Some friends.'

She packed her camera carefully back into her orange rucksack.

'That's got to be the winner.' She was happy, waiting for me to drive again.

We pulled in for breakfast just past the Navajo Bridge which had replaced the ferry service. The place was crowded with Germans ordering big breakfasts in loud voices. We hugged the bar counter, waiting a long time for French toast. Martha tried the paper stall in the foyer as we left but they didn't take anything from Flagstaff.

'Guess I'll miss our centenary photograph.'

As we climbed up to the North Rim of the canyon the trees climbed down again. Ponderosa pine and spruce thickened to a forest that guided the road from open parched desert to high boreal forest in a few short miles.

Meadows opened out where the water table rose high enough to prevent the pines from seeding. Thick grass filled hollows with patches of snow still hiding under the pines in stubborn drifts. The flow of change consumed our attention. A deer thudded across the road fifty yards in front. Three or four skulked just beyond the fringe of trees, waiting for the car to pass.

We had joined a small convoy that lengthened to a queue at the entrance of the National Park. Ten dollars paid for unlimited access over three days.

The road snaked on, fringing the edge and offering glimpses of the chasm below. Cars and campers pulled over in lay-bys; Americans on a day off. A great country for driving around. The radio informed us that thirty million would be on the road that weekend making journeys of thirty miles or more. The canyon, though, didn't seem that crowded.

We picked a promontory at random, parked the car and followed a marked path to the edge.

An American couple joked that they were going to take the twelve-second tour. It was a long way down.

The rock shimmered in all shades of red, filling the sides of the chasm cut through by the Colorado river that had now disappeared in the distance of its base. I read the information sheets trying to make some sense of the confused geology. A huge expanse of time splayed out to see: layered in red sandstone. It was so easy, effective because it was imaginable. The sandstone that holds up the hills around the South Wales coast is of the same age, give or take a few million, but the hills are green and round with fields and sheep that hide the scales of time, clothing in human terms. It is abstract. Imaginable but not visible.

Here on the North Rim the whole vast expanse of measurable time was splayed out, exposed to the imagination in bed after bed of horizontal rock descending to the base. Then underlined by the cut of the river which was so very recent, almost ephemeral compared to the rock, a mere twenty million years old, but it could be imagined, it was there, erosion was still sculpting the canyon in recent rockfalls from the preceding Winter, while the whole age of human life could be measured in the thin soils that supported the pines. Trees triple the age of any human wondering about time.

Flights of cliff swallows twisted over the great chasm, chasing insects on the thermals that billowed up from below. We watched them for an hour before walking back to the car.

A sign warned about lightning strikes in late afternoon.

The Visitor and Information Center was bustling; loads of visitors but little information. A fine-looking restaurant was closed for the afternoon. A church service was being held in the meeting hall. A handful of pious people were seeking friendship and confirmation.

A map suggested another route down to the rim seventy kilometres south, fifty over unmetalled road. I wanted to see the river close again.

The road skirted the park as it turned south, edging over into Utah for a few miles before going back into Arizona.

Just past Fredonia we stopped at a gas station. A man pushed a bicycle up to the bench where we were sharing a coke. He was tired but wanted to talk. It had been a long straight day on the road.

Further East, driving high across the panhandle, I had passed pairs of cyclists pushing hard from the west along the flat straight roads.

They appeared incongruous, somehow out of place on the lonely grasslands that ached for a fast car. Often a small flag fluttered on an aerial behind them. It was usually the yellow and black of the German Republic, sometimes the

Dutch, occasionally the Union Jack. The flags somehow explained the madness; Europeans on a cross-continent trek taking the quiet road and avoiding the big trailers.

A roadhouse owner in Hardesty reckoned he saw two or three a week in the season.

'They kind of cheer up the place.'

But Paul Walsh was a genuine American long-distance cyclist. He lived on the coast at Big Sur but this was his third cross country trip and he was filling in the gaps he'd missed on the last two. He was heading for the canyon.

'Maybe two days away. I'm aiming to get there after the holiday. Most Americans just don't understand long-distance cycling, it's just too weird.'

He was a quiet, careful man who deliberated over each question before delivering slow, careful answers.

'I sort of needed the break. I told the guys at work either they give me five months or I'm leaving. They offered me the Winter but who wants to cycle in the Winter? Big Sur's nice but I don't want to stay there every Summer.'

He gave the impression that cycling was therapy for the summer. Big open roads, repetitive motion.

Martha continued talking to him while I walked up into the town looking for a store. Late lazy Sunday Afternoon, Memorial Day weekend. Nothing open.

When I returned Paul had already gone.

'He said sorry he had to get moving, needed to find a pitch before dark. Look, he gave me this book.' Martha thrust a tattered paperback towards me, *A River Runs Through It* by Norman Maclean; 'reckons it's a good read.'

I fingered the worn pages. Someone had enjoyed reading it.

'The film was boring.'

Martha looked at me in disgust, as if I was a spoiled child at a party.

'Sorry.'

'Yeh well, you ought to read it now.'

'I will, sorry.'

We drive on looking for a road back to the canyon. The highway thins, then a sign points east across a dry, treeless plain. The tarmac gives up and the car thuds to the rough, ribbed surface of a graded road.

'How far to go ?'

She ruffled through a torn map trying to make sense of the distances.

'Fifty kilometres.'

The car rattled its disapproval. I try slowing down but at ten kilometres per hour it is going to take a long five hours to get there. I accelerate to forty and feel I am going to shake into pieces. I will need the car after tonight.

Twenty kilometres on I give up. A faint dusk is sheltering the plain. We haven't passed another vehicle. A wake of dust drifts out across the grassland following the line of the road.

'We're camping here ?'

'Yeh, the car was going to shake to pieces.'

'Shame.'

We didn't bother pitching the tent. It was a warm night and the blankets were enough to soften the parched grass. Martha wouldn't believe I could pick out satellites between the stars. I found four before she relented. I even pointed out a planet that could have been Mars but I didn't really want to sleep anyway.

I woke first in the morning and watched as Martha gradually stirred. She had a line of red marks pierced into the side of her temple where a mosquito had feasted in the night.

Her eyes opened slowly, then widened with a brief panic as she focused up. Then she turned away.

'Its early.'

It took me twenty minutes to convince her sex was a good way to get into the day.

A wooden sign fifty yards up the track pointed to Turner's Pond. It was an uninviting looking pool, smelling of drought and drying mud around its fringes. Turtle tracks led off onto the grassland. I wondered where they thought they were going. A kestrel skimmed the bank looking for dragonflies or lizards before disappearing over the rise.

The water was thick; cloudy with dust and stillness. A green weed covered the bottom clinging to submerged branches in swollen slippery fronds.

We swam out of habit; easy strokes keeping us above the weed. The only sounds the light splash of water breaking the surface. We quickly returned to the shore; sharing a towel to dry.

'Not the Colorado.'

'No.'

'Vegas today ?'

She looked at me. I guess she was deciding things.

'Yeh, I guess.'

We drove back to the highway. This time I pushed the car to fifty and we began to plane. The road smooth at speed; but now it was smooth running south.

The highway curled along the Arizona border before brushing again into Utah at its southern edge. The road ran through Hurricane, a Mormon town culled from the desert. Another small, sleepy town but with a religious zeal that oozed out of the clean white houses.

We stopped for breakfast at the Miracles Café. A rare vegetarian restaurant open early on a holiday morning. The menu special was scrambled tofu. The cooking smelled fine and they were playing Michelle Shocked on the radio. We relaxed into it.

On the wall was a framed page of the *New York Times* that carried a story on the white flight out of California to the desert states of Nevada and Utah.

A long, reasoned piece on the problems of the influx. New ideas, new customs. The words "Hippy Café in Hurricane" were highlighted, placing the Miracles in print.

There were rumours and figures for a new breed of migrant; people giving up the life on the Coast and heading back East over the border to the wide-open spaces of the desert states.

They claimed there were too many problems in California, too many drugs, traffic, smog, drive-bys, guns, people.

Small towns such as Hurricane were becoming the new frontier in a new dream.

They were fleeing the Mexicans, the Guatemalans, the Vietnamese, the blacks. Anybody not white and affluent.

Settlers arrived with money and ideas, not too many were retiring. They brought their own problems with them.

They were bored; the new towns needed a bit of excitement, a bit more nightlife, more movie theatres, more drive-through restaurants. More like California, in towns where the major social focus was the weekly church meeting.

Discipline was becoming a problem in schools. The children of new migrants were proving a disruptive influence. Standards were higher in Utah. Friction was inevitable.

There was concern over the imminent arrival of two men from San Francisco who intended to run a wholefood store. The implication was that they were a couple. The local people were unsure of the need for more lentils and bean curd but a recent arrival was quoted,

'That's just what this town needs, two old faggots from Castro.'

The owner of the Miracles was discussing plans with her architect for a new shopping mall and integrated restaurant complex.

I drank a second cappuccino and pretended not to listen. The owner had big ideas. This place was going to make her a lot of money. More money than the pile she already had. Franchises, national food chains, all promised a big return.

The Sunday papers arrived, a date late but the regulars squabbled over the assorted sections of the *Los Angeles Times*. I guess there weren't too many articles on community life in Hurricane.

On the way out of town we pulled over at a yard sale. Three families had pooled their junk and were making a few extra dollars at give-away prices on the weekend.

A young girl asked twenty-five cents for a paperback.

Martha rummaged but bought nothing. She looked disappointed that there was no bargain to hold her interest.

Breakfast in Vegas

Give me that breakfast, $2.99 as many turns as you like. Eat now spend later. We don't close here.

The art of all-you-can-eat America surfaces in one expressionist feeding frenzy high in the Nevada desert. Las Vegas, gambling on nothing in a rush of cheap food, hotels, and beer. Sustained by a collective urge to bet and perhaps win something back from the American dream.

If you haven't made it yet try Vegas for one last throw on the strip. Or if you're on the way down, one last booking. The halls are alive with dying stars real and imaginary; as an entertainer you need never die, just become impersonated. Nobody knows the difference; Roy Orbison, Ray Charles - who's alive ? Who's dead ? Who cares ?

There's $3.7 million paid to slot players every day in just one of the casinos. I listen as my two dollar share of it tumbles out into the well. I look covetously at my winnings; I'm part of it, I want more. I feed the machine.

Along the row Ed Night is winning more than I am. His well rattles to another five dollar pay-out. We're not playing the big machines, where the turn of a disc can spill ten thousand. This is safe; the tables scare me as the only game I can understand is roulette and that only partly.

Ed's flown in from New England but when he hears my accent he mentions he's originally from Bedford, laying on the Cockney slang for my benefit.

'Are you from Ireland ?'

He'd been in the States forty years.

'Been back once, thirty years ago; never now; it would have changed too much.'

He first came to Vegas back in the 'sixties when it was still a small town huddled together around the main boulevard. Now it's sprawled out into the desert, forcing back the sage brush and stones in an attempt to make even more money.

Ed had been playing the small machines all afternoon.

'I don't take it too seriously, don't win much, don't lose much. The drink is cheaper here, reckon I'm four dollars down on the machine but six up on the drink, that makes me two clear.'

He enjoys Vegas, considers it a good thing, but he's concerned about the spread of casinos across the country.

'It's okay here, it's controlled but gambling brings crime. Even in the East we're getting bingo and casino malls opening up, usually on the Indian reservations.'

The Indian Nations have been some of the more enthusiastic supporters of nationwide gambling, which their own laws allow to develop in prohibited States. It's also tax-free. Some tribes are at last becoming rich, becoming part of the America that has excluded them for so long.

Ed tells me some stories of big wins which seem unreal as we both feed the dime machines and I roll on my way to losing a hefty seven dollars before lunch.

The unreality of it all is one of the keys to the success of the city. People come here expecting to lose money and they are not disappointed. This then becomes reality and is presented in a number of guises. A St.Louis paddle-steamer lies stranded in the desert as if abandoned by some long-forgotten flood of the Mississippi. Its quarterly steam horn rebounds across the strip as if in warning to the captain of the rocks that lie ahead.

Water is obviously the key to a conscious need in the desert as across the five-lane freeway lies Treasure Island. Resplendent with palm trees, bleached skeletons and chests of doubloons which sparkle in the sunshine, the island lures unwary buccaneers with offers of a Spanish King's ransom. Adding to the spectacle, a pair of galleons in full sail float in a huge lagoon which completes the island's seclusion. Throughout the afternoon the galleons sail across the water, enacting a pitched battle with cutlasses and canons as they skirmish their way into the minds and pockets of the castaways struggling eagerly ashore. The ships fly the Skull and Cross-bones.

This is a simple ploy of diverting attention to the real prize of the wealth inside; once distracted, the cool interiors of excitement, noise and slick, alluring nature of machines, tables and cocktail waitresses will perform the rest.

Caesar's Palace doesn't need this easy approach; its attention is guaranteed. It has the name, the reputation, the big acts. As much as any one hotel can be it is Vegas. Caesar's: where the money is.

The survivors of the wreck are not allowed through the front door with the big rollers, but are moved leisurely through a wide plaza on flowing escalators followed by a soft voice that promises wealth and riches.

A group of Japanese men ahead of me on the escalator throw nickels into the fountains which fringe the plaza. Wishing for luck, they will need it.

Once through the gates of Rome the gambling is postponed. A wide boulevard of white marble leads up to the palace gates. People drink, buy clothes, watch grotesque statues revolve and talk. Midas dances beneath a painted sky of blue and light, awaiting expectant applause.

The message is hidden but obvious and relished. This is Caesar's; this is Rome. A palace where gods dance and fortunes are made by a simple touch. This is reality, this is now. A life of dreams is only the turn of a dice away; the spin of a machine. If you tire of the excess, the Nile flows and Cleopatra sings from her barge.

Later, as I leave, three women, long, beautiful and tired, scuttle out of the palace gates into a waiting chariot numbered Caesar's Eight. Five men eager for the pleasure they have paid for ease after them into the air-conditioned comfort of the stretch limousine.

Pass on By

Vegas was not my kind of town. We arrived late on a holiday Monday, only there are no real holidays in Vegas.

The hotel was big, bold and soulless; clean, conditioned rooms packing them in at forty dollars a double.

I didn't care the first night. The first night was more of Martha. A big double bed, red covers and curtains, a round bath squeezing two. Vegas still playing on, waiting, expectant, flaring through the window in bursts of sound and strip lighting. It was good from the 11th floor, standing naked in the dark of the room, her body bathed in shadows and darkness, soft tight curves that my hands moved slowly around and under.

Early in the morning we watched an old movie play in

black and white. The voices were clear, strong. Emotions given willingly to a studio camera still playing to a hotel room in Vegas.

James Cagney was playing a gangster with a conscience, down on his luck returning from the war and making a little money bootlegging. We waited for Bogart to appear and he

didn't disappoint us. He was playing the bad guy. I didn't recognise the actress but Cagney was calling her Panama. Her fine figure captured without mortality. Cagney was up to kill Bogart and somehow reprieve himself.

Martha fell asleep towards the end but I waited until

Panama closed with the line, 'He used to be a big shot,' as Cagney lay dying in her arms after the final shootout.

We slumbered on late into the morning. I closed the curtains to hide the clear desert, trying to lengthen the night. A room-cleaner hammered through into a dream. I had been on a wide beach south of Avalon. Martha was still lying with me but I was in Vegas and sex had given me an appetite.

The dining hall was scarred with the signs of a massacre. All you could eat for $2-99 and the hungry hordes had gorged through. Squashed sausages and toast, scattered cereals all lying around on the red tile floor. Long lines of canteen food stretching for a hundred metres to the cashiers. A few late risers chose between congealed crusty eggs, limp bacon fragments and the odd apple. Every conceivable breakfast food had been available and wrenched from the counters. We shared a bowl of fruit and a packet of cornflakes each.

'We're between shifts right now, kids.'

The waitress smiled at us as we searched for a clean table in the wreckage of the dining hall. She served us our one obligatory coffee and then returned to fawn over a Japanese couple on honeymoon. I guess we weren't a good bet for a big tip.

We watched as the machine began gearing for the lunch-time frenzy.

The first casino was fun. Martha was pulled in by the offer of a free mug. She waited patiently in the queue for her blue and white porcelain freebie. A notice above the counter boasted that over six million people had been mugged in Vegas.

The gaming rooms were big and airy, filling up even before lunchtime with people eager to feed the machines. I changed ten dollars into nickels, split half with Martha, picked up a complimentary plastic money pot and we played.

A constant ring of money falling into the other wells heightened the levels of our greed.

A big win was twenty dollars.

Waitresses in short taffeta skirts and fish-net tights haunted the alleys with offers of cheap bacardi or gin. We ordered for the hell of it; the bacardi was weak with rapidly melting ice and left a sour taste in my mouth. Martha ordered another two and drank mine.

'Got to get the atmosphere right.'

'I'm just warming up, tonight it's Caesar's.'

'You play the tables ?'

I winked at her.

After an hour I was bored. Martha refused another drink but she was beaming.

'How're you doing?'

I looked down into my plastic pot, which had become considerably lighter.

'I reckon I'm down three fifty.' The machines are clever. They drip-feed winning lines to keep the gullible humans interested. They know you're in no rush to go anywhere; this is Vegas. Sure, there are signs proclaiming how many million dollars are paid to slot players every day but the machines are always on the make.

'I'm up three bucks.'

'Yeh.'

'Call it a day ?'

'On three bucks?'

'Sure, I'm winning.'

'Ok, let me lose the rest of this.'

We walked along the main highway. Vegas prospered; shiny happy people holidaying in the sun. Massed hotels fought a long duel, with hoardings and flashing signs as the weapons of combat. Ridiculous cabaret acts at thirty dollars a seat.

'Hey, look at those bums.' Martha pointed at a full-colour advert for a male dance troupe called 'The Thunder from Down Under'. Glistening torsos oiled to perfection muscled out of the picture. 'They were just making it in Brisbane before I left, went to see them with a couple of the girls.'

'You paid for it ?'

'Sure, they loved themselves but it was a laugh. Dana got off with one of them after the show. She could never live it down but claimed he was a good shag.'

I looked to see if she was kidding but she seemed serious enough, laughing to herself about the memory. I looked up at the boys beaming down from some Australian beach, now performing in a Vegas club. Which one ?

The hoardings continued. The Righteous Brothers looked out hopefully through a facefull of skin lifted and stretched, not quite believing they were still up there performing. Would they sell enough seats for another season at the MGM Grand? Their skulls seemed to be shining through, impatient for a go at the real world.

Mirrors under the sun

Old Trails Inn

Every offer was for a seat, an act, a tour. Diversions to the real time. Gambling time.

By midday people scuttled between the cool havens of air-conditioning avoiding the open spaces.

We paused outside the Frontier Hotel, where a recorded rhyming message hailed through an insistent public address system implored gamblers not to support "the mean greedy owners, be on the right side and stay on the outside, hold your head up high and pass it on by." The hotel was being buffeted by a protracted union dispute, and a frontline of committed activists manned a sun-shelter outside the main entrance. The loudspeaker did most of their public relations, even offering a list of alternative hotels where the management were more friendly and less greedy. Where there was a good time to be had gambling.

The Frontier had been bought by an heiress from out of town who had promptly imposed new conditions and working practices. Non-union practices, below the minimum wage, longer hours. The staff had walked out en masse, even the Head Chef. The Head Chef seemed to be some sort of prize and ultimate moral victory; if the Head Chef goes, they must be bastards.

The Frontier had found some new staff but the dispute was on and the union stuck to it. The city authorities had become involved; backing the union. Other unions had supported a boycott. There were not too many people to put the management side. I guess they didn't have much of a side to put. A stubborn boss used to getting her own way with money coming up against a committed union organization.

The hotel still had some business but the guests were being harassed and only the pig-headed bastards enjoyed being called a scab on their two-week vacation in Vegas. The owner wasn't winning many friends but I don't suppose she really cared.

'We've been out for over a year. Most of us have found work in the other hotels but we keep this going for a settlement.' A young, dark-skinned woman ventured briefly from her sun-shelter to talk to us.

They wanted compensation and it looked like they they were going to get it.

'I'm expecting a lot of back pay, enough to get me out of Vegas.'

The case rumbled on through the mire of the civil courts and, if the management were found to have broken the employment laws, they were going to be forced to pay out a huge sum in accumulated backwages.

By midday most of the pickets allowed the speaker to man the line but a lone activist remained just outside the forecourt of the Frontier, ambushing anyone who dared cross into the hotel, his voice rasping through a loud hailer.

'Walk on by, leave the Frontier alone. It's a poor place; the food is poor, the staff are mean; stay out; there's a hundred better places on the strip. Hey you, sir, you're wasting your money, pass it on by.'

There was an intensity to his passion that was fascinating.

'That guy's crazy,' Martha pointed at him. It was nearing one hundred degrees. He was whiter than the others, dressed in shorts and t-shirt while the sun bounced off his balding head. Stains of sweat darkened his clothes. Even the other strikers appeared to regard him as an oddity. The guests or gamblers unwise enough to enter by the main lobby recoiled from his powerful, untiring invective. He was possessed.

We paused to watch his performance. His commitment merging into fanaticism; compelling.

'Money-waster, pass this hotel by.'

As if he was locked into a duel with the recorded voice to see who would tire first.

Byron

We waited at a stoplight to cross Las Vegas Boulevard into Treasure Island. The battle of the galleons was about to begin in the lagoon. A crowd lingered, despite the heat, for a free performance.

'Hey, Martha.' A voice boomed across from the group waiting on the far sidewalk. We both looked across.

'Martha.' The man was waving to be sure we had noticed. He could have saved himself the trouble. Half of Vegas heard him.

'Shit.'

I looked at her. 'Who's that?'

'Byron.'

'I guess you know him.'

'Yeh.' She shrunk into her shoulders.

'Martha.'

She waved back to shut him up. People on the sidewalk had begun staring at us.

'He's my boyfriend.'

My eyes opened. A shudder into my spine, muscles tightening.

'Look, I was going to tell you, last night, tonight. I swear I was. I just didn't get around to it. Thought we'd be able to avoid him for a day at least.'

'Avoid him ? You mean you knew he was going to be here ?'

'Yeh, sort of.'

The lights had changed and the group surrounding us had moved out across the road. Byron was running from the far side.

'Look, be cool alright.'

'Yeh, sure.'

Galloping Byron was almost upon us. He started his conversation from twenty yards.

'Martha, where the fuck have you been? I been looking all over.' His Strine was as deep as Sydney Harbour. 'I bin sick with worry, you crazy woman. Told me you were going to Vegas and here you are. Could have killed you the last couple of days.' He was angry but it was overwhelmed with relief as he wrapped a big hairy arm around Martha's waist, lifting her effortlessly.

'Should have believed me, Byron.'

'Yeh, you always told me that, but I found you again now, you crazy woman.' He was tall, lumbering and happy. Then he noticed me.

'Hey, who's this guy ?'

I smiled at him, my best long friendly smile that tried to confirm every suspicion he might ever hold about me. Martha began to explain.

'He hasn't been making up to you, has he? He's been alright, has he?' His tone darkened as he placed Martha back down on the sidewalk.

'Don't be stupid, Byron.'

'Cause if he has.' He straightened himself a little further, glaring at me. I cranked my smile and lifted an eyebrow. He looked dull enough to try something. Out there on the sidewalk in a hundred degrees.

'What you been up to, mate ?'

I'm not sure how I would have answered that one but Martha cut in again.

'He's just been helpful that's all, given me a lift here, you daft lunk. Don't you trust me?' There was an accusation and a threat all rolled so closely together that Byron was left with only one answer.

'Why, 'course I do Martha, just, you know.'

'What ?'

'I just thought, girl on the road. I was worried, just worried, that's all.'

She smiled him a reprieve. 'Where you staying anyway?'

'KOA; I've been there three days, looking all over Vegas for you. Even been to the police, they weren't interested, just filled in another missing person's file and told me there's thousands of them.'

The Mississippi paddleship sounded its steamhorn to mark the hour and the crowd on the far side of the road cheered as the galleons set sail. I was beginning to feel the heat.

'You coming then ?'

Martha looked at me and I shrugged my shoulders.

'Where we staying again?' She smiled at him. He didn't understand why.

'The KOA.'

'Give me the address and I'll meet you in an hour.'

'What the fuck for? I got the car in a lot just over there.'

'I just got to say goodbye.'

'I'll say goodbye for you. Goodbye, mate.' He bared a thick set of white teeth at me. A sidewalk crowd had gathered for the free show this side of the strip. They looked on with interest.

'Don't be an arsehole Byron, he's been very nice.'

'Well, just say goodbye and we're gone.'

'What's the address ?'

'Martha, I don't fucking believe you.'

She stared at him, standing a couple of paces away before extending her open palm towards him.

'Shit.' He fumbled in the pockets of his jeans; finding a card, he passed it to her.

'An hour.'

She kissed him on the cheek. 'I hope it's got a swimming pool,' then touched his arse with her hand.

'Yeh sure it has.'

'I'll be in it then, see you in an hour.'

I was about to say my fond farewells to Byron when the lights changed again and Martha pulled me across the road.

'Didn't say much ?'

'I was being cool.'

We sat in the beach bar of Treasure Island drinking cheap rum and coke.

'So you just walked out on him at the gas station?'

She fiddled with a pink plastic umbrella, stirring the ice

into water.

'We had stopped for a pizza and he was just getting a bit too much. Sometimes you just need a break. Step out of things. Slide over to another life.' She dropped a square of ice into her mouth before cracking it sharply with her teeth. 'I'd been on the road with him for fourteen months.'

'Was he in London with you ?'

'Yeh and before that, Thailand. He's from Brisbane too, or a little place just outside of it.'

'Right.'

'Look, I should have told you but we were having too much fun.'

'Yeh.' The rum was making the afternoon go a little quicker but I still had problems with a smile. 'So you're going on with him?'

'Yeh, Byron's alright really, you just saw the raw side of him.' She looked at me and we both laughed.

'We've got a flight out of San Francisco in August, back to good old Oz.'

'Don't suppose I'll be visiting you there then ?'

'Why sure, come along. Byron just love to have you for a barbie.' She deepened her accent for effect.

'It's been fun.'

'Yeh.' She curled back her lips, leaning across to kiss me. 'It would have been good with you, I'm sure, but you can't try all the roads.'

Vegas kinda lost some of its sparkle when Martha caught a cab to the KOA. I offered to drive her over but I'd been drinking too much rum by then. I hung around in the beach bar for a few more bacardi, slipping through the afternoon. I lost more money on the machines before walking up and down the strip watching people. Caesar's cheered me up for a few more drinks, the money beginning to spin. I watched a couple of good 'ole Southern boys shout on a short fella called Barnie, who only just made it high enough to peer over the baccarat table. He was on a winning streak and they were backing him with enough enthusiasm to bust the bank.

'C'mon Barnie.'

Barnie didn't seem to mind the attention but he didn't play to it either. He rolled the dice tight with concentration as his supporters cheered him on to another win. Other players watched with interest as Barnie in his khaki suit cut for a safari captured the attention of the hall. A waiter arrived with more drinks as his chips grew; the Southern boys drank eagerly; Barnie just kept on throwing.

The blaze of the casino making money fired around me. A woman with brown hair and bright, red lipstick sat across the table. She appeared bored but smiled nicely as I drank more cheap, clear alcohol. She was from the East selling software at a computer fair. Vegas was apparently a favourite location for business. Plenty of distractions. We danced through the usual questions about accent and motive. She was married but alone. Her lips had a way of expanding when she smiled that I found appealing. She was a good story-teller and I was listening.

'There was this guy in the casino yesterday. He was dragging one of those drip-feed life supports around with him. What they called ?'

I just shrugged.

'If you could only have talked to him that would have been a story. I mean he must have been really ill and he still wanted to play.'

She seemed to find the whole mystery intriguing. A man near death forcing himself around the machines for one last go. I found the evening a possibility. My mind moved again to her lips but I had drunk too many bacardis and my words were merging. She smiled again as she left for her hotel. I ordered another drink.

The hotel room hadn't changed. Big and red with an enormous double. Vegas played on beyond the window. Still moving fast in a rush of light and noise.

I woke early in the morning and my hangover thudded in with the light. The tv still playing to the movie channel.

> Cars float by
>   On a blue tide
> Free from the world
>   Wanting in.
>   Seeing smiles that I know
>   In faces that are
>   Strangers.
>   I drift.

Needles

I abandoned Vegas the next morning as soon as my hangover agreed to co-operate. The city seemed to stretch a long way out into the desert but eventually the casinos and shopping malls gave way to a series of harsh canyons and arid saltpans as the road ran south.

Thunderstorms gathered in the distance but no rain fell to wash the new dust off my car.

The radio coursed from channel to channel as I tried to avoid country and mournful songs about lost love. A man on the highway asked for a lift and I surprised myself by stopping.

His name was Tai and he'd been up in Utah working on a Mormon study camp.

'Liked the hills but not the religion.'

He was heading back home to Santa Cruz on the West Coast, where his father lived. His mother was in the East; he seemed unsure where he was going to end up.

'May be South America. I want to study Spanish in college.'

We talked of hitchhiking, then travelling as the road fell south through arid canyons to Needles. He'd been to Europe on a world tour. He hadn't liked London.

'People assume this attitude once they know you're American.'

Needles came up suddenly, sheltering on a bend of the Colorado. The river was slower, wider and I guess a lot warmer. The town looked much the same as any other, supermarkets grafted onto the I-40 at the edge, the center wide and deserted.

We found a bar on Broadway to sit out the rising heat over food and a beer. The bar is empty save for us and the barmaid.

'Jack should be in around one; he'll tell you what it's like to live around here.'

I gazed across to the value store which dominated the center of Needles. In twenty minutes they had two customers. A police-car cruised by looking for entertainment. Nothing else moved. Jack was ten minutes late.

'You'll have to speak up son, my hearing is not what it was.'

I adjusted the volume.

'The heat? You should be around here when summer really starts.'

The waitress disappeared into the kitchen. Tai bought another drink. By three we were still going nowhere.

Jack reckoned I should go and visit the Old Trails Inn. I wasn't keen but I didn't want to hurt his feelings. He offered to walk me over. Tai was still looking out onto Broadway.

'I think I'll stay the night here. Jack reckons there's a campsite on a hill outside town.'

I think Tai thought the heat had got to me but he didn't appear to relish the thought of walking out to the highway again. He pulled a paperback out of his bag and settled back to read.

'I'll wait here for you.'

Jack guided me across Broadway. The sun bounced off the pavement; no movement; everything seemed congealed in the heat. Three blocks down a white hotel proclaimed its name as the Old Trails Inn.

'Hank owns it, just tell him Jack sent you.'

Hank Wilder was a mechanic who had retired from fixing

cars to run a hotel on the route he had worked on all his life. Encouraged by a growing interest in the history of 66, which ran through the center of Needles, he had rescued a dilapidated hotel and restored it back to the 'thirties.

'I was working in town during the 'fifties, there was a lot more poor people on the road then. And the cars, you should have seen the cars. The country wasn't nearly as affluent as it is now.'

He was charging $33 a night, which seemed good value for rooms stuffed with real 'thirties furniture and radios that played voices from sixty years ago.

'In my day there were still a lot of Okies on the road, travelling back and forth from California, visiting relatives back home or maybe they'd given California a go and decided it was better back home. They couldn't settle down. Guess most of them are long gone now. Still go out on the highway myself in the summer, take the wife up to Flagstaff when we get a chance.'

He pushed a switch and a voice he claimed was Fibber Magee crackled out of a wireless set.

'Sure takes you back.'

I walked back to meet Tai. The church on Broadway rebounded out of a photograph on the wall of the Old Trails Inn. It didn't seem to have aged.

The diner was empty.

'Said to tell you he was going to give the road another try. Said thanks for the lift.'

The road out of town finally finds the campsite perched on a hill above the Colorado river. The reception is closed until six. A couple of children splash in the pool guarded by a mother asleep in a lounger. Everything else is still. I struggle with the tent, pegging it under the mottled shade of an eucalyptus.

I'm the only one moving on the site when an RV towing a white Volkswagen Beetle with wide-rim tyres pulls across the gravel.

I wait out the heat for an hour in the shade. As the shadows lengthen people begin to move around the site. I introduce myself to the owners of the Beetle.

Richard and May Nilo who are on their way to California for another summer. They were going to visit an old friend and planned to stay a few months to help around the house.

'We call her that old lady but she's fifteen years younger than us.'

'She's all alone now,' added May. 'Last Summer we painted her whole house.'

The Beetle was adapted for off-road exploring around the mine workings that lay abandoned near their own Arizona home.

'A two-bit town, down across the Colorado river.'

Calling themselves Snowbirds, they were migrants from Canada who had stayed when they came South in the 'forties. He'd been a mechanic and a fireman and many things in between. He asked about the UK, concerned if there was a problem with violence.

'It's the guns, any fool can buy them here.'

He was going to get an early start in the morning. Make the hill up into the Mojave before the sun got too hot. It was a big hill. His wife couldn't help him to drive any more due to failing eyesight.

'After you've gone she's going to ask me what you look like.'

I laugh as she squints up and peers closely at my face; only an inch away.

'You look okay.'

I rise early in the morning hoping to see them but they have already gone. I hope they have a good summer in California. It was hard to imagine one without the other. As May remarked.

"He has to stay alive to take care of me."

Richard was eighty, May seventy-nine.

Germans, The World Cup, and Language

From the first week in July I began meeting wandering groups of heavy white Europeans who could only have been Germans. They were eating breakfast in the Grand Canyon Diner, playing poker at Las Vegas, swimming in the waves at Big Sur, admiring the trees at Sequoia, watching fish in the Monterey Aquarium. They travelled around in tour coaches or were driving big, expensive hire cars. They all spoke with thick guttural accents that enunciated a fluent if unique English.

I talked to a rich American from Oregon on a fishing holiday deep in the Baja Sur. He was friendly and genial, buying me two rounds of coke. He even knew where Wales was and liked Richard Burton. He thought I spoke English very well. I thanked him for the compliment. After all, I've spent twenty-seven years perfecting it with only a two-year foray into French at school and several aborted attempts at learning the first language of my father. Nothing forces me. I can get by. From Spanish package tours as an eight-year-old to a month's bus ride through Thailand, people will speak or understand English. The white Europeans with big smiles and big handshakes are usually German, sometimes Dutch, and will always speak a fluent English. It is a language they have absorbed not just to communicate with Americans and British but with almost anyone else they might need to converse with, from Sinhalese shopkeepers in Galle to that French couple windsurfing in Essouira. It is the world language.

Australia, that Mecca for young affluent educated Europeans with nothing better to do than travel for a few years, is a useful language school, French, Swedes, Norwegians, Italians all drifting through a dozen faceless hostels practising fluent English. The British and the Irish join in.

The UK is tied to this success and it cannot escape being absolved into a lazy mono-lingual tongue, American by association.

But the world will be at least bilingual. World communication will be in English but the real deals will be brokered in Spanish or Mandarin or Japanese or a dozen other incomprehensible tongues to the monoglot Americans and their small neighbour an ocean away.

America is on the verge of legislating a monolingual society. A white élite, nervous of their privileged position, are trying to stem the growth of a bilingual education. The white Europeans lost their language early. The darker people to the south stayed closer to their heritage and a stronger culture that is now beginning to re-assert itself. California, that State of the ultimate American dream. The Golden state on the coast will soon become majority Spanish-speaking.

The Germans lost unexpectedly in the Quarter-final and thousands of supporters had another week touring Southern California without the prospect of a winning final on a warm Sunday afternoon in July. They didn't seem to mind; there was always the next one. At least they could speak the language.

The Mojave in the morning is bright, yellow, and empty like the deserts in the stories. I come off I-40 and follow Sixty Six again. A Californian State sign informed me that it is now Historic Route 66.

Halfway across the final desert before the sea I stopped in Amboy pulled in by another café out of the 'fifties.

This was another town the new road had avoided, leaving it adrift on a high volcanic plateau. I ordered eggs but the cook had to be summoned from her studio where she doubled as an artist. She made it clear that I was an inconvenience. I talked to the waitress who proved to be her sister and friendly. Her sibling fumed over the eggs in the kitchen.

'I'm not the regular waitress, I'm only helping her out while she finds someone regular.'

She was from Albuquerque and had only planned to stay a few days as a favour. It was now near a month and her husband had been spending his time counting the railcars on the Santa Fé Line as they pushed east.

The eggs were good despite the cook. A German couple on a motorbike replaced me at the bar as I thanked her for the coffee.

'There were a hundred and nine cars on that train,' remarked her husband as he sold me five dollars of gas from the single pump on the forecourt.

'That's the fourth through this morning.'

After Amboy 66 loses confidence with the size of the

Mojave and rejoins I40. The traffic is thick with trucks and RVs climbing slowly west. But I've grown confident with the Honda and it glides easily on, the needle on the temperature gauge holding a steady mid-point.

Then the road dips, the desert fades into the fringes of Barstow and the Mojave is almost over. I get lost in Barstow. I want to head out along 58 but get confused by the signs in the center of town. A policeman on a motorcycle indicates that I should pull over.

'You ran a stop sign back there.'

'Sorry.'

'Hey where you from?'

He asks to see my documents then directs me to 58.

'Guess you don't have them over there.'

On the slip road out of Barstow I recognize a figure on the highway. He runs to catch up with the car.

'Hey I missed you.'

Tai collapses into the front seat again.

'Didn't get very far then.'

'I got across to here last night but I just couldn't get going this morning.' He picks a grass stalk out of his hair in the mirror.

'Rough night ?'

'Could say that.'

We talk for a while, then run out of things to say. A Stealth Bomber flying low over the desert prompts a few more words.

'Guess we must be near Edwards, the airforce used to deny those planes ever existed.'

He relaxes into the movement of the car and quickly falls asleep. I wonder if this is the usual effect I have on my passengers.

The road continues on. There is one last climb through Southern outriders of the Sierra Nevada at Tehachapi. The slopes of the hills have been cleared of trees and replaced with forests of wind-generators that turned lazily in a weak breeze. Then the land dropped sharply away to the long, flat San Joaquin valley that glistened with irrigated water. Huge acreage of tightly-controlled agriculture spread out under a heat haze to the north. This was the land that attracted generations of migrants as the promised land on the coast.

A sign on the highway outside Bakersfield extends an invitation to today's migrants.

"Come for a visit stay a lifetime"

Tai gets out at the next junction. 'Bakersfield's my least favourite place, it's boring.'

But I decide to accept the first part of the invitation.

The Big Trip East

When the first flush of uprooted farmers began appearing in the long, prosperous valleys of Central California, John Steinbeck was a struggling writer living in a run-down one-bedroom house with a leaking roof while the wind whistled through the cracks in the boards.

In his home town of Salinas itinerant migrants were becoming a common sight as they roamed the State in search of employment on the vast factory farms. A squatter camp had settled on the fringes becoming known as Little Oklahoma. Steinbeck sensed there was a story in their lives.

A decade later he would recall a story about a trip he made East to research the book that made him famous. A long trip over the desert and plains to Oklahoma. A journey he made with Tom Collins, an employee of the Californian State Resettlement Programme, it would provide Steinbeck with much of the detail that coloured his novel. He would tell the story to his new friends, friends from a new world of Hollywood and New York socialites while attending dinner parties given by his soon-to-be-second ex-wife. He was always vague about the details; sometimes he would tell the story as a joke on himself. He had only got as far as Needles on the California-Arizona border.

His early books had been ignored as he shuffled from one publisher to the next and remaindered stock gathered dust in forgotten warehouses. He lived simply, collaborating with his wife, Carol, in a life that gave him freedom to write within the constraints of obscurity.

His first break came with the acceptance of a novel by a committed Eastern publisher who had been recommended his early work and undertook to bring out *Tortilla Flat* with a contract for more.

The book was a small success: a satirical account of dead-beats on the shoreline at Monterey, it sold well on the West Coast. Steinbeck was pleased with the money, even making a sale to the movies, but he wanted to move quickly away from a reputation as a satirist. He was looking for a subject, a serious subject.

He pushed on with a book about union organization in the picking fields. *In Dubious Battle* portrayed an enduring picture of workers being exploited by powerful monopoly-controlling farmers. It had moderate sales and a lot of criticism from the Associated Farmers who accused him of being a Communist sympathiser. He was beginning to lose his obscurity and at first he hated it.

'I was not made for success, I find myself now with a growing reputation. In many ways it is a terrible thing.'

In August 1936 he was asked by the editor of the *San Francisco News* to write a series of articles on migrant farm labour in the San Joaquin Valley. He was guided around by the Resettlement Administration, who were keen to promote their programme of government-organized camps. Tom Collins was the first camp manager. There were an estimated 70,000 migrants in the San Joaquin Valley.

Steinbeck realized the subject he had to write about was pouring into California in their thousands, driving beat-up old wagons they flogged across Route 66 with that dream of a better life on the coast.

The Long Valley

Bakersfield had been strangled by a thick vine of freeways that had flourished around the town. I missed two exits before 58 swung north onto 99.

Near the edge I followed signs for a campground. The noise of the road faded quickly as I pulled into the gravel bedded park. The only sound was a light, high whirr of propellers as a crop-sprayer coated the lines of fruit trees that stretched out across the valley.

It was another KOA, half-full with RVs sheltering from the sun under a line of poplars. The facilities included showers, a laundry and a swimming pool for eighteen dollars a night. Camping had moved a long way from the desperate pitching of thousands of migrants in the thirties.

The new camp manager was cutting timber for a brace of log cabins he was building in the deepest shade next to an apple orchard. The plane drifted down on the trees again. Another RV pulled across the grass towing a Morris Minor.

The driver was on his way back to Silicon Valley after five months in the east visiting relatives. I didn't get his name but he was easy enough to talk to. He'd been in Europe during the war as a wireless operator but had never been back and seemed more concerned with tales of his travelling than any reminiscence over his military days.

'The wife's got five sisters spread all over, one here in Bakersfield, another in Fresno and a couple in Miami. We like to get an' see them once a year or so.'

The parts were hard to get for the Morris but he was in the owners' club.

'Sold up the house a few years back when all the kids left; bought into a mobile home co-operative up in the valley. We've had no rent increases for seven years.'

He'd retired fifteen years ago and was looking forward to at least another ten on the road.

The rich used to retire when they got old in America. Now they hit the road funded by thirty years of accumulated pension contributions, investments in equity and a comprehensive health care policy. Another life. More time to amble, talk and watch the seasons drift by in fifty states.

'Seen forty-seven, Missouri, Michigan and Ohio to go. Maybe next Summer.'

People were moving slow.

I waited for the heat to slip back into the afternoon before pitching the tent. The pool was warm and open until sunset. It was an evening for not doing anything much. Just watch the camp, the smoke of barbecue and children playing.

Buck Owens Owns a Radio Station

As I drive back into town on the freeway, the morning is filled with a smooth efficiency of people making a living. Trailers and saloons crowding the road but moving fast.

Bakersfield sprawls out to meet the fields along the ribbons of road that run straight and flat up and down the San Joaquin Valley.

The center of town is low-rise with wide streets that are half-filled with cars but empty of people. A few figures scuttle between offices but there's no rush hour. The main business is further out, where air-conditioned malls sell everything.

The Union Hotel stands on Hoborn Street. It boasts a preservation society which keeps it standing. It's a rambling hulk of a building, offering shelter to a handful of businesses, including the obligatory diner, a hardware store, a barber's and a book exchange. The diner is full with pensioners, white and tired-looking, while the barber's offers reductions all week for elderly citizens.

I get lucky first time.

'Sure, my dad was an Okie, came over just before the war, lived in Bel Gardens just south of Los Angeles, used to call it Billy Goat acres account of all the Arkies and Okies living there, but I think that's what they always called streets with a family or two from anywhere East, not very original around here.' He raised his voice to attract the attention of a trio of pensioners at the other end of the breakfast bar. 'Hear what I say? Not very original around here.'

The trio mumbled among themselves but decided not to take up the challenge.

'See what I mean ?' The man returned his attention to me. 'Yes, Okies and Arkies, grew up speaking like I was from Oklahoma City and I never been further East than Barstow, 'course where we used to live, that's all changed. Big ethnic change, mostly Spanish-speaking there now. All the Okies and Arkies moved on to some place else.'

He called over another coffee from the waitress. 'Tell you who you should talk to.' He nodded slowly to emphasise the necessity of his advice. 'Buck Owens, he used to play in a famous bar down in Bel Gardens called the Chit Chat. He owns a radio station and tv station right here in Bakersfield. I think it's forty-six or five.' He tried to confirm it to himself before consulting his friends.

'What channel is it ?' He shouted over to the listening trio.

'Forty-five.'

'Yeh, forty-five. He came over with his family in the 'thirties when they didn't have two dimes between them, got involved with all that country music and now he's got his own station. What I understand, he's a real friendly guy. I'm sure he'd talk to you.'

Bakersfield seemed friendly but Buck Owens had no free appointments for a week. The state was embroiled within the preliminaries for an election later in the summer. The first wild claims were being made. Immigration was again the issue

The San Joaquin Valley had been at the center of the migrant influx during the 'thirties, attracted by the promise of harvesting work in the huge farms that flourished on the fertile soil. It was here that many of the people first realised the dreams they had used to sustain a long trip West; dreams of owning land again and making their own way in farming were only dreams.

The valley was already owned, divided and organized along ruthlessly efficient lines to maximize profit through industrial production. The people from the East were another cheap resource, a glut that forced wages down boosting profit margins further over a short harvest season.

The numbers overwhelmed the work and the available accommodation. Some of the larger farms provided temporary shacks for seasonal workers, for which they charged exorbitant rents and forced tenants to buy food at inflated prices through company-controlled stores.

Families spilled out to the edge of towns, where they were forced to set up squatter camps on any spare land they could grab. Usually they were just on the fringe of a highway or hugging the banks of a dried river bed.

They had nowhere to go. Back East was a sold-up share lot or a failed business.

The private and public reaction to the migrants was of resentment shading to open hostility. But the sheer numbers involved in the migration made it impossible to ignore and the State Department of Rural Rehabilitation, following the recommendation of an economics professor called Paul S.

Taylor, promised a state-wide construction programme of organized camps to absorb the influx. The proposal was immediately opposed by the United Farmers, who distrusted any form of labor organization, presumably on the premise that it would make the workforce more difficult to control.

The scheme did finally get started, funded federally but with a much-reduced programme that only suggested a small number of demonstration camps. The first was established in Maryville and the second on the fringe of Bakersfield at Weedpatch. The first camp manager was Tom Collins, who would establish and help run all the early migrant camps.

Collins was a humane and generous man who had a background in the priesthood and education in the army. On leaving the service he founded a school for delinquent boys which although ultimately unsuccessful further strengthened his ideas on social justice. He moved on to work for the Federal Transient Service during the early years of the depression, where he organized vast soup-kitchens to feed the growing numbers of transients floundering in urban poverty, washed up by the economy.

He was an idealist who knew the realities the migrants faced and became a highly-successful camp manager, introducing administration regimes that were based on self-governing committees in an attempt to re-build the self-esteem of a people abused by years of hostility and dislocation on the road in California.

He had ambitions as a writer and made copious notes on the rhythms of life in the camps, which he submitted as weekly reports to his employers, including detailed personal histories, dialogue extracts and even short stories. John Steinbeck first met him at Weedpatch.

'*The first time I met Tom Collins it was evening, and it was raining. I drove into the migrant camp, the wheels of the car throwing muddy water. The lines of sodden, dripping tents stretched away from me into the darkness. The temporary office was crowded with damp men and women, just standing under a roof, and sitting at a littered table was Tom Collins, a little man in a damp, frayed, white suit. The crowding people looked at him all the time. Just stood and looked at him. He had a small moustache, his greying, black hair stood up on his head like the quills of a frightened porcupine, and his large, dark eyes, tired beyond sleepiness, the kind of tired that won't let you sleep even if you have time and a bed.*'

The two men developed a quick, easy friendship as Collins explained to Steinbeck the workings of the camp and the philosophy behind it. Over the course of several days at Weedpatch, Steinbeck attended meetings, watched the progress of the Good Neighbours Society, even went to the camp dance at the weekend. He visited the unofficial camps which littered the fringes of Bakersfield and he met the people living in the camps and working in the fields. All in the research of the articles he was writing for the *San Francisco News*.

When he returned north to work on a feature that would eventually become 'Their Blood is Strong' he carried with him a sheaf of written reports supplied by Collins that would form the detailed basis for *The Grapes of Wrath*. He had been impressed with the reports when he first read them at Weedpatch and initially proposed a collaboration with Collins.

'I've been thinking a great deal about the collaboration work. Been reading such of your reports as I have. They are a magnificent collection. So fine that I couldn't hope to equal them. Consequently, I should like to present the following plan for your consideration. That I take these reports - edit them, rewrite some but keep them consecutive - cut out the private matter and the figures - maintain and include the human stories. There is drama and immediacy in these things. I should reduce them almost to the form of a diary; iron out any roughness - write an explanatory preface and see to publication. It would make one of the greatest and most authentic and hopeful human documents I know of... I can act as editor or possibly in a sense as synchroniser. And I can get it a hearing. That is the main thing my name can accomplish.'

The book he would eventually write was still two years away and it would have Collins's name in it but it would be as part of a simple dedication.

'To Carol who willed it and Tom who lived it.'

Steinbeck met Collins several times over the next two years, including a further research journey into migrants which became the Big Trip East that he would later boast about but he did very little with the manuscript apart from read it and pass it on, first to his agent and secondly to his publisher.

With the publication and favourable critical reception *Of Mice and Men* he began to sense that the success he had been striving for was building but with it the unwanted partner of fame. His books were becoming widely-read but, with it, the growing cult of the personality began to follow him. He moved to a ranch outside Los Gatos in an attempt to preserve his anonymity but Charlie Chaplin drove up to the house and introduced himself; Hollywood was on the phone.

The book continued to ferment and people continued to search the valley for work. Two years later as he started his own work on *The Grapes of Wrath* he wrote back to Collins to end their proposed collaboration.

'I knew that I was not a good editor, so I sent your reports to the best editor I know, Pascal Covici. His reply disheartens me a great deal. He says that no Eastern publisher will touch the reports, first because they are sectional and not of general interest, second because to give them the completeness they would need to be of social significance would cost so much, and third because no house could sell enough copies to break even. Were it any man but Covici I should say bunk and go on with the plans. But Covici is the head of the only socially minded publishing house in the country... I wish I didn't believe it but I do... The thing that hurts me is that I had hoped from this piece of work which I still think is the finest social study I've seen, you could make a little money to carry on with.'

Steinbeck was pulling away from Collins but he had not finished with his reports. Whole sections of Collins' work, the immediacy and drama of which he had praised two years earlier, would find its way into print but not as an acknowledged collaboration.

Steinbeck suggested that Collins might try a different form. Collins attempted to write a novel. Several years and numerous redrafts later a book was accepted by a West Coast publisher. Steinbeck wrote the preface. It attracted poor advance sales and the publishers pulled out.

Steinbeck began writing the book that would become *The Grapes of Wrath* in the Spring of 1938. It followed the fortunes of the Joad family from Sallisaw in eastern Oklahoma West along route 66, through the desert states of New Mexico and Arizona, before finally arriving in the San Joaquin Valley. Here they become one of thousands of rootless migrants drifting from one short-term picking job to another. Living in squatter settlements, government camps and even the tied labour camps provided by some of the larger farmers. The plight of the family which gradually disintegrates is portrayed against what Steinbeck saw as the larger destruction of the American rural way of life. Of small farmers, foreclosed and tractored out by the ruthless efficiency of agribusiness.

He completed the book in one long draft which was immediately edited and typed by his wife and true collaborator, Carol. They finished together in the fall of 1938, Carol finding the title from a line in 'The Battle Hymn of the Republic' late in the production of the manuscript.

'To Carol who willed it...'

It would mark the end of the most vital period of his writing life.

Covici, the publisher who had brought out his previous couple of books, including *Of Mice and Men,* had recently been declared bankrupt but fortunately for Steinbeck the company had been rescued by Viking and took the author with him as the coming man. *Grapes* would receive the the full publicity backing of one of the strongest publishing houses in America

The book surfaced to a storm of praise, harsh criticism and publicity. The sales were immediately enormous. Steinbeck would soon be a rich man and fêted by the fame which followed hard on the rush of good fortune.

'The telegrams and telephone, all day long speak, speak, speak, like hungry birds. Why the hell do people insist on speaking ?'

The world wanted a piece of his success, a success that arrived with a force that frightened, overwhelmed and fundamentally changed the man. From the moment the novel was published in April 1939, Steinbeck was on the run to another life. A life of New York socialising, meetings with the president, Hollywood friends. He abandoned the ranch to Carol; they would separate within a year. The book sold 200,000 copies in the first month while the film rights were auctioned for $75,000. He headed south to Hollywood.

Shortly after the filming of *The Grapes of Wrath*, Collins, who had secured a job as an adviser with the production crew, called to see Steinbeck at his Los Gatos home. Much of the location filming for the John Ford production had been carried out at Weedpatch and at other locations suggested by the former camp-manager. Collins had been writing regularly to Steinbeck on the progress of the filming; who had in reality ceased to care. He commented on the picture to Collins in a short note: *'Saw the picture and it is swell. You did a wonderful job on Grapes.'*

When Collins reached the house he found it boarded up. The two men never met again.

'To Tom who lived it.'

ॐ

I found Weedpatch easily. Its name had been ironed into the map just south of Arvin. The fields are still controlled by the Associated Farmers and workers still endure long hours in the hot fields. But the Okies and Arkies have gone, merged completely into the huge American economy that was kick-started by the war and burgeoned into affluence in the great consumer rush that America has become.

A country of success where the world continues to trust an uncertain future.

With *The Grapes of Wrath* John Steinbeck articulated for a generation of white Americans the experience of migration and the dislocation that accompanied it. He wrote out of reality, a reality that was supplied by Tom Collins and his own observation of life in the fields of the San Joaquin. But the book created many myths, myths furthered by the movie and then forgotten by the war. California has always been a state of migration, and a state of agriculture dependent on cheap, seasonal labour. The Okies and Arkies temporarily filled a vacuum created by the forced relocation of thousands of American citizens in the early 'thirties based on the premise that they looked Mexican and spoke Spanish. Mexican Americans with citizenship rights through birth were persuaded and threatened to return South across a fluctuating border. Rumours of Mexicans living off welfare paid for by the tax-paying white citizens of America were spread to make their expulsion easier. Employers erected signs stipulating White-labour only. The Southern Pacific Railroad ran a weekly train out of Los Angeles loaded with

Mexican-Americans for the cost of one week's relief payment per person. It was a brutally simple solution to unemployment.

Earlier attempts at controlling immigration had been frustrated by the Growers' Associations and the expanding railroads, who needed the cheap and malleable source of labour but in the 'thirties there was a new supply driving in from the East. They were silent for a while. They guessed the workers would still come but they would have fewer rights.

The workers have always been seen as migrants and the truth is always easier buried in an old book about the fundamental strength of the American people who overcome a long trek to reach the promised land. There are no Okies working long hours in the fields. But the workers are still there.

In the early morning around Bakersfield and Arvin groups of men and women still head out into the fields on the back of beat-up pick-ups or crammed into battered, rusting Fords. Some are migrants while some are citizens but they are all working long hours for poor wages.

Today the migration is from the South. It is a long tradition from a group of people who had farmed and owned California long before a disparate band of American settlers began a ruthless usurpation. Weedpatch is now called Buena Vista and the neighbourhood is one of the many Spanish-speaking enclaves that provide life and work to the state. The shopping mall offers immigration advice and Spanish video stores, but the fieldworkers are again perceived as the unwanted outsiders.

California has a migrant problem. Many of the migrants work in the fields. Agriculture is still the intensely-controlled precision production that relies on cheap labour to harvest. The Valley hasn't changed that much. Today, as they always were, many of the fieldworkers are Spanish-speaking, tracing an American descent from before the Bear Flag revolution. But everyone not white is a migrant.

The radio and newspapers are filled with the first, dark predictions of the coming election. The election issue will be immigration. Migrants are being blamed for a state full of problems.

I listen and watch.

The North

'We come here to work.'

This is a claim Palo Reyes feels he still has to make after living in and around California's San Joaquin Valley for twenty-six years. It is a claim he thought his three children, two in college, one working, would never need to make. They are citizens by right of birth; he has yet to make the pledge.

The badge of citizenship has become a token of American belief that is being championed by pilgrims and recent arrivals as a cipher of conformity. Are you a citizen ? Vote now, Save our State from the hordes of illegals.

The scenario is simple. California has a problem; too many people, too few jobs. A recession of sorts. People still believe in the American ideal; prosperity, freedom. It exists.

Enter the Alien. Illegal aliens; thousands of them are pouring across the broken borders in the South, from Mexico, from Guatemala, from Nicaragua. They are all heading North, stealing jobs, living off welfare, avoiding taxes, claiming benefits that are paid for by the tax-paying citizens of the North. You can believe this; it is on the screen. Tenebrous black and white images of the Border at Tijuana. Cars stalled at the checkpoint, the American side. Suddenly an explosion of people, dark-skinned people clutching belongings, running desperately up the freeway. Running to the North. Enough, the commentary says, Save our State, vote for Pete Wilson, the Republican choice. He will stop this.

Easy rhetoric, easy targets.

Migration West or North has always been part of America. Over one million people still chance their future in the great pot every year. California more than any other state is closer to this history. It has gorged and grown fat on people, absorbing migrants from all cultures. Palo Reyes is part of this history as he is part of America and part of Mexico. There are no clear definitions across a line through the desert that passes for a border.

The border is both real and imaginary depending on whom you are talking to. For wealthy businessmen it no longer exists; free trade is booming as Mexico climbs to America's second most important trading partner, forcing its way into the economic premier league. However, for a twenty-year-old Oaxacan temporarily camped on the fringe of Tijuana watching the lights of San Diego sparkle only a run across the patrolled exclusion zone, the border is as real as the money you've spent getting this far.

It is the people on the border that the advocates of Save Our State intend to halt. They are the easiest targets but their aim extends further.

Save Our State

The SOS was announced in the spring of 1994. In a well-funded campaign orchestrated by Alan Nelson, who was head of the Immigration and Naturalisation Service under Ronald Reagan, and his West Coast minion, Harold Ezell, it was quickly endorsed by the struggling state governor Pete Wilson.

Its professed key objective is to reduce the motivation for immigrants to travel to the U.S. by denying them state benefits that were guaranteed to all residents by the state constitution. All publicly-funded health and social services excepting medical care will become unavailable to people who cannot prove citizenship, legal residency, or lawful temporary status. In addition, suspected undocumented immigrants applying for such support will be reported to the Immigration and Naturalisation Service.

Perhaps the most dispiriting aspect of the legislation is that it will attempt to deny an education to the children of undocumented workers. It is here California aims to step backward in producing a racially-determined, poorly-educated working class only allowed a menial role at the table of American Prosperity.

The idea behind the SOS is no more elegant than enough is enough. It is not even original. The last trains carrying immigrants back south left Los Angeles sixty years ago but some people can clearly remember the repatriation purges. Welfare assistance was denied and the state passed a law in 1931 making it illegal to employ aliens on public works programmes. The definition of aliens was flexible. Nobody is calling for wholesale repatriation now; the execution needs to be more subtle.

But the ideas are there; bolster the Border Patrol with the National Guard (El Paso, Texas). Charge a crossing fee at the border using the money to bolster the Border Patrol (Tijuana/San Diego). Introduce identity cards. Threaten

Mexico with sanctions if they don't do their share. The basic tenets are the same; blame somebody else. Keep the illegals out, the legal uncomfortable and yourself out of the line of fire and in office.

The campaign fought within the heightened reality of the media screen fired the imagination and prejudices of a portion of the people that were struggling to come to terms with the reality of California as bilingual. A state that will soon become majority Spanish-speaking tracing a common heritage to the South. And a South that begins in California and Texas and New Mexico. This is and always has been their country. Soon they will control it again.

This is believed and related by a mass of white emigrants heading out to the desert states of Utah and Nevada, supporting stories of a white flight avoiding ethnic diversity. Moving out to Hurricane.

I talked to a couple in a bar on the coast at Encinitas. They were moving to Utah with a scheme of running an environmental bookshop.

'We were becoming uneasy with a racially-controlled State, there's going to be a big change in attitudes here and we don't want to be part of it.'

Southern California looked affluent from the safety of the bar. The couple drink cocktails with friends and select their words carefully. They were all Californians but their friends' parents had spent part of the war growing up in an internment camp for Japanese-Americans.

'The place has become too tense, too strung out.'

They believed the media predictions of a higher crime-rate as normal living became ever more precarious, based on the influx of immigrants. Belief and truth are not the same; the truth is more subtle, less dramatic.

The state will become a majority of Spanish-speaking Americans, many of whom might not even bother to vote. There are some middle-class prospectors, mostly white, heading for the hills, but there are more driving in on Interstate 40. California is in a flux, which it has been since the Spanish established a chain of missions along the coast in the last decades of the Eighteenth century.

But it is SOS that has put immigration back on the political altar and it is Pete Wilson who has successfully climbed on with it.

But Palo Reyes makes the most obvious remark that exposes SOS for what it is.

We come here to Work

People migrate for many reasons but the greatest number will always migrate to find work.

The suggestion that the majority of illegal immigrants who enter California have come to sit on their butts while making a fortune off state benefits belies the basic misunderstanding that anyone sitting on their butts making a fortune has about welfare claimants. Sure it is possible to find the occasional Tijuana teenager who has vaulted the fence in order to have her baby in America and hence ensure the child's opportunity to have an education. Education, that common, everyday commodity, almost worthless unless it's a luxury.

The people not considered a threat are those who have travelled two thousand miles from Oaxaca, spent all their savings and are now working twelve hours a day picking strawberries in a field outside Santa Cruz. They have to work and the employment a large number of immigrants have traditionally been able to secure is supporting the huge Californian agricultural industry.

It is an area that Spanish-speaking Americans have found strength, in their numbers, in the nature of their work and their role as supportive pawns in a business that generates huge profits, provides rows of cheap food on the shelf at Wal-Mart but pays a necessarily seasonal and transient workforce as little as it can.

'These people are the poorest paid in the country. They have no contracts, they have no rights or the rights are ignored.'

Magdaleno Avila is a union man. He has to be; there is no pay in the Union. Organize.

The Union

A thin, young singer in a band of thin, young musicians is attempting to instill some movement into the listless audience who edge further away from the stage.

A strange place for a gig. A cluster of date palms on a spare lot of a supermarket, Mecca, Southern California.

It has been another day in the field; no one is ready for dancing. Most of the crowd will have been working ten hours, picking grapes in a heat that would stall in the low hundreds by mid-morning. The temperature is now falling but the date palms that provide the stage an amphitheatre of sorts only offer a thin veil from the sun. People in narrow lines, west to east, following the shade trunks, make the best of things. Soon the singer will finish, ushered off by polite clapping, and the speeches will begin.

The United Farm Workers are not at their lowest ebb; that was last year. Last year Cesar died.

Formed in the mid-'sixties by a committed group of activists of whom Cesar Chavez was a leading member, the United Farm Workers mounted successful campaigns for Union representation, minimum wage agreements and safety standard improvements with many of the growers' organizations that dominate agriculture in the San Joaquin Valley.

Chavez had been born into a poor farming family near Yuma, Arizona. His father's land had been grubbed out by the depression, forcing the family onto the road in an effort to find seasonal work in the factory farms of California. He wrested an education out of a series of scattered schools before serving a short term in the United States Navy. Returning to the migrant life, he became involved with a Community Service Organization that worked for civil rights improvements for Mexican-Americans. Through this he began advocating ideas for the Union Organisation of Farm workers but when his proposals were constantly rejected by a conservative establishment he resigned to concentrate on setting up a union by his own efforts. By 1965 he had built a core of support around the Delano area. A core of organisers that were willing to support a long strike for Union recognition in the fields.

In August 1965, another small union based on immigrant Filipinos struck for higher wages in the Delano vineyards. When the growers tried to break the strike through using Mexican workers, Chavez called for a ballot. On the 16th of September, Mexican Independence day, after

Lewis Davies

a unanimous result, the Delano Grape Strike began. It was the defining moment for the Fieldworkers' Movement.

The strike received huge publicity and considerable support from a wide spectrum of public and private bodies. It struggled through to the Spring of 1966, when during a march through the valley, the growers' organization with whom they had been in dispute finally agreed to a modest wage increase and the principle of collective union bargaining. The union burgeoned, flushed with the optimism of success.

Through effective use of boycotts and selective strikes over the following decade, it was able to mobilize large-scale public support, forcing other employers to negotiate and sign contracts. Laws were advocated and passed. The Agricultural Labor Relations Act of 1975 finally included agricultural workers into Union America, forty years after they were specifically excluded by the pro-union Wagner Act. The Union expanded from a few thousand to over a hundred thousand members at the peak of its influence in the early 'eighties.

People are less willing to talk of its decline but the last ten years have not been a good decade. National legislation and a Republican state administration hostile to union involvement in industry played a part but the Union accepts some of the responsibility that saw its membership fall to under twenty thousand. Perhaps it lost some of its direction, becoming embroiled in a media-marketing exercise that attempted to polish an image in a culture that excluded its own members. It was fine having learned articles penned in the *Los Angeles Times* but not many field-workers had subscriptions.

The nadir arrived with the death on April 9 of Cesar

174

Chavez, their leader and visionary for twenty years.

'We let Cesar do too much.'

The tributes poured in. The congressional Medal of Honor a recent addition. He was a man of stature who had raised the profile and aspirations of a whole community. The growers waited for his Union to die quietly with him. But his death has proved a catalyst in forcing the Union to re-examine its direction and influence. The Union is going back to the fields. Every worker is an organizer.

In April of 1994 it mounted a march from Delano to the state capital of Sacramento. Three hundred and forty-three miles through the agricultural heartland of the San Joaquin Valley a recognition of the first one thirty years before. The growers were dismissive; Jack Pandol of the Association called it a publicity stunt, but fifteen thousand joined along the route.

The march was a commemoration, beginning on the date of Cesar's birth, ending a year after his death, but more importantly it became a pledge to the continued support for the ideals of Cesar and a vindication of his promise of faith.

'I would not spend one hour organizing this union if I thought it was going to die when I die.'

Most of the crowd under the date palms at Mecca have come to listen to what the Union might do for them. The majority are not even union members; this is also a recruiting drive. The meeting is buoyed by the recent signing of a contract with the David Freedman Company, one of the biggest growers in the area. The president is going to speak.

Mecca lies at the center of an agricultural area in the far south east of California on the shores of the Salton Sea.

Close to the Mexican border and an easy access across the desert, the land balances on the edge of aridity. Ten miles either way, the tightly-controlled fields of vines and watermelon fade quickly into stone and sage brush.

A number of speakers precede the key-speech by Arturo Rodriguez. The tone is cautious; they know they are asking a lot. Subscription is twenty dollars, which is sometimes a day's pay. Many workers are only over for the summer; when the picking ends they will slip back across the border to Mexico. The long-term benefits are hard to see: many will have listened to and believed Cesar in the 'sixties, when he promised better conditions and better pay. And for a while the promises came true but now Cesar is dead and the contracts have lapsed.

They are still the lowest-paid workers in the country. The growers fail to provide adequate sanitation out in the fields; they are charged for transport, have to buy their own tools and company shops over-charge. Cesar complained about pesticides in the 'seventies; now there are cancer clusters in farm-worker communities.

Rodriguez begins like a man on a long road. He knows the crowd, he knows the growers. The growers have the fields and the money. The people need the work. He knows his members often find work more difficult to secure. Nobody wants to employ a union man unless he has to. Sometimes they are physically intimidated. The Union honours five martyrs. Twenty dollars is twenty dollars. But the crowd like him and he grows more confident, he mentions the Freedman contract and they cheer. He promises more contracts and more improvements but they must join. They must understand what they are fighting for; who they are fighting against.

Finally opening out the issue he mentions SOS. The crowd hiss; they know this concerns them now. The attacks are personal by people who can afford to pay for television adverts. People who can collect six hundred thousand signatures that forced the initiative onto the November ballot.

SOS is such an effective emotional monogram. It is easy to understand who they are trying to save it from. SOS means keep the Mexicans out.

There is loud applause as Rodriguez denounces Pete Wilson. The architects of SOS may be able to escape the consequences of the proposition but Wilson's name is going to be irrevocably linked with an idea whose basic premise will divide a state along ethnic lines.

But ultimately its effectiveness may not be in its success in denying education but in focusing an essentially homogeneous people on a Spanish-speaking political agenda.

The figures are ominous for the Republicans. Thirty million people identify themselves as Hispanic in California, representing twenty-eight per cent of the state's population, but at present only ten per cent of those are registered to vote. It is projected that 425,000 people will pledge citizenship this year. Doris Meissner is Clinton's head of the INS; she is clear on the benefits of citizenship.

'The naturalisation process is a continuing re-affirmation that newcomers want to join up, that they do, by and large, share the values that those of us who came before share.'

The key idea is assimilation; America wants to feel itself as a whole. The people who came from the East have always found it easiest to assimilate, forget their past, lose their identity in the flat tones of a white English language. The people from the south have always been seen as Mexicans.

'Do you think they can speak English ?'

It is an embittered question, loosely directed by a man who waits his turn in a queue lengthened by people he doesn't recognize as his own colour. A job center in Bakersfield doubling as a benefit office is as unremarkable as any other. Thin scuffed carpets, plastic chairs, information posted to white walls. In a dream of prosperity, some people have stalled on the road west. SOS has given them someone to blame.

Wilson bases his support on the cost to the state of the criminal element of illegal immigrants. Figures suggesting foreign national inmates in State jails cost 370 million dollars annually have prompted Wilson to issue a law suit against Clinton's administration for direct financial support for these prisoners under the premise that immigration control is Washington's responsibility. The case has little chance of success but that is not its objective; Washington, in its remoteness, is also a fair target.

Wilson's law suit follows eagerly the emotional SOS charge that the state is supporting a vast population of illegal immigrants who are claiming unemployment relief, food stamps, medicine and receiving the horror of a free education. This is a free country but you have to pay for everything.

The initial success of SOS is that it has encouraged a basic misunderstanding of the reasons why immigrants travel to the United States in the first place. To earn money; become part of the American economy.

'This is a successful country, people want to come here.

Who can blame them ?'

Roberto de la Rosa works for La Raza, a support agency helping recent immigrants of any nationality and the promotion of leadership initiatives within the Mexican-American community .

'We're getting too old, the young men must take some of the responsibility for our people, Chicano spirit.'

To him SOS is a campaign of hate. He is aware of the problems recent immigrants face but he is proud of the contribution they make to his country. The Urban Institute in Washington estimates that recent immigrants, legal and illegal contribute $30 billion dollars annually while a study in Los Angeles County on illegal immigrants estimates they provided a cash injection of $4.3 billion into the economy in 1991-92 while costing it only $947 million in support payment.

Clearly immigration pays and it is a cash payment: in a state fixated by credit purchase, the rating of an illegal migrant from Oaxaca does not trouble a Visa account. Payment is in cash now.

Also the last thing a recent arrival wants is to be detected by the INS; he or she is unlikely to risk this in a written language they may not understand.

Pete Wilson is too knowledgeable a politician not to understand this. His supporters in the agriculture business are aware of the realities. They know undocumented workers will still travel north in search of work but if SOS passes they'll have fewer rights and will cost less. Opinion polls indicate that a majority of Californians also rationalize that the new immigrants take jobs that no one else wants. Analysis of Welfare claims confirms a skew away from Spanish-speaking recipients; both white and black sections of the community have higher percentages of claimants.

But despite the facts, SOS was building a fierce momentum during the heat of a long Summer. In one of the world's most privileged areas the dream has stalled; not everyone is a millionaire. Someone needs to be blamed.

'This SOS is aimed at us, but maybe first we need to feel the hits, the pain before we start to realize.'

Educate, Organize

Woodville is one more stop on the road for Roberto De La Rosa. A card game across the grass has drawn almost as many people as the La Raza meeting but he is not disheartened. He knows the people who have come to listen will talk to others. What he needs to do is motivate.

Woodville was established by Tulare County as a workers' camp but has the feel of the permanent village it has become, with a school, community center and a wide, tree-fringed green where the card game and La Raza meeting compete with a kids' game of soccer despite Mexico's loss during the afternoon to an unheard-of East European team.

He asks if everyone has heard of SOS. The term is well-known.

'What I'm going to do is tell you how it is going to affect you.'

The people listen intently as he emphasizes the practicality of its proposals.

'That child there, when she starts in school, she'll have to take a paper around her neck to prove who her parents are. What if you can't find the documents? Next year all the children will have to prove who they are.'

It is this denial of education that De La Rosa is most worried about.

'If they take away our schools they take away our future.'

In a country that is essentially an immigrant community, the provision of a state-funded education has become one of the cherished statutes. It will be a step back in the state's history.

But the real urgency for La Rosa is that many of the people whom it will affect are not able to vote. The supporters of SOS do not worry about offending anyone. The people who are targeted don't count; they are a minority.

Most of the people at the meeting have legal residency in America through years of earning a living in the fields of the San Joaquin Valley. But when asked who can vote, only three hands rise and Palo Reyes is not one of them. For to vote you have to be a citizen, and to be a citizen you have to pass a written examination in English on the perceived history of the United States. If you believe you are living in a state that was stolen from you in the first place, this is a harder crossing than the deep scar which still marks the border.

It is these people who will be affected by the new police powers to co-operate with the INS.

'The suspicion must be logical, it'll be men of my colour who will be stopped.'

He points to the only anglo-looking face in the crowd.

'The police when they stop someone for identification to find if they're legal, they won't be stopping him.'

Three days later I'm driving up from San Diego on Interstate Five. There is a police checkpoint studying all traffic on the freeway. Five cars slip through before they urge a battered chevy to pull over. Its two occupants merge with whatever a police identikit of an illegal must tell them to look for. They look Hispanic. Everyone else drives through.

Last Summer an INS patrol followed a man driving a pick-up truck near the border at Pamona. He was wearing overalls and fitted their description of a recent illegal immigrant. When he was stopped for questioning and challenged to produce some identification the officers found they had apprehended the town's mayor. The apologies were profuse and hurried.

The Border

Tijuana is the border pushing in on America's imagination. Grey steel fences and a barren strip of land littered with rubbish and wrecked cars marks the agreement of signatures on paper. This is the busiest international border in the world. Thousands of tourists and commuters stray across the line every day, twenty million legally every year.

San Diego is a city powered on cheap immigrant labour. Work consists of long shifts in factories and kitchens. The wages are low but they are higher than what is available on their own side. Tijuana is a night out, tequila and excitement. Under-age drinking. Clothes and cheap videos crowd the narrow streets with people. Prices are displayed in American dollars. A town on the make, feeding on the scraps from its rich neighbour.

But Tijuana is also a last stop for many on a long travail from the south. This is where the money begins to run out, leached by the the higher prices even while America is frustratingly visible. Border guides charge enormous fees to smuggle people across. There is no money-back guarantee only a night in custody and a free meal from the Border Patrol if caught.

On the Californian side the freeway south tunnels into a controlled zone. Stern metal fences crowd the highway, yellow signs warn of illegals running free on the road.

The signs picture three people in flight. They are not Americans. A man pulling a woman pulling a child. It is the artist's impression of the threat. A threat that is being poured onto the tv screens.

People running. Dark-skinned people. The music heightens the tension. This is a siege. This is America.

Cars flow easily down the five-lane freeway that runs through the suburbs of San Diego straight to the border. The control post south is hardly manned. There is no toll. No checking of passports. Why waste money ? No one is escaping into Mexico. On the Mexican side cars pile up to file slowly through the checkpoint. Children sell brightly coloured jewelry and woollen rugs to tourists idling in the traffic. Big American guards check passports or wave cars through depending on license plates and colour. Another myth, south is escape.

But on the road that skirts Tijuana, the people in the signs on the northern side are there in reality. They stand in the bright heat of the summer, peering over the grey fence, planning a route on. They hold all their possessions in their hands. Tied ragged bundles or battered hold-alls are enough to carry everything to the North.

Once across it might be easier to merge. But the emphasis is on colour. Do you look illegal ?

Where you from ?

Dave White is from Southall. He is a big man, his face and muscled arms are tanned but his London accent has yet to soften. He doesn't look like a man who could merge easily anywhere He's casual and illegal but work is available.

'The only thing anyone's asked me for is a tip.' He's been in the States for three years. 'I've been back, but I'm not going back if you know what I mean.'

He works three to four days a week labouring for another Dave from Adelaide.

'We paint decks, four hundred dollars a week cash.' They both play rugby for Los Gatos at the weekends.

'There are ways in. Last time I came through Canada on a holiday permit. You've got to be careful. A mate following got busted back to Australia.'

Los Gatos is a town filled with an easy wealth. But there are other sides to that wealth.

'You see the Mexicans waiting on the corner of the yard where we pick our paint up, they'll work for ten dollars a day. I don't think anybody's asking for no green card.'

Without identification and being the wrong colour

many people will be finding themselves on an expenses-paid trip to the border. It will be a cosmetic exercise. This is not a serious attempt to stop immigration. Border Patrols will remain a futile gloss manning a fence that fades into the desert twenty kilometres from Tijuana. People will still travel to search for work in industries that depend on low-wage labour. But now any benefits will be denied. Benefits that migrants working fifteen hours a day for $3 an hour are already paying for in tax deducted at source.

Wilson is aware of the reasons to keep the border open. Perhaps his biggest financial contributors are in Agribusiness, a business more dependent on migrant labour than any other but they are not alone. Los Angeles is another city increasingly functioning through the efforts of recent migrants in low-skill low-wage industrial jobs. The restaurant trade would collapse without its Spanish-speaking employees. Mexico itself benefits substantially from worker remittances; the money earned in the North is important as a capital source used to set up small businesses or build homes. The result threatened to force immigration to the front of a National Agenda. There were a lot of eyes on the election.

The promotion of 187 seemed to reflect a wider retreat inward of the American intelligence to a position of no interest in the larger world as long as there's a personal road West following a great tide of manifest prosperity.

The economic reality appears different, as ever forging its own path. *The Los Angeles Times* ran a week's feature on ethnic diversity while McDonald's advertises in Spanish on billboards outside Fresno. It is a future that is heavily linked to Mexico.

But in concentrating on a negative image of their own

privileged existence affluent supporters of SOS. revealed a perception of the world which looms as a dark, miasmic swamp of unstable dictators and desperate immigrants fighting to reach prosperous American shores. California seemed to understand only a vision of an isolationist utopia while supporting a measure that ignored the contribution of a huge number of its lowest paid workers.

But ignorance will not frustrate the future, it will be a diverse future. There is no other.

The voices and the people absorbed me as I continued with the road. *The Grapes of Wrath* was a book fifty years old and there were still people on the edge, working the fields. Steinbeck had moved on to another life funded by success in his first. The crops still needed to be picked.

I gradually edged north; more campsites, more trailer parks and RVers. Ninety Nine followed the fall of the valley in thick lines of irrigated agriculture. Sprays of water pushed life into the fields, swelling with summer heat: feeding easily on the thick, fertilised soil.

I listened to the radio and read papers in a succession of bulging libraries. I love the half-silence of books and people reading.

I met a biker from Texas who assumed I was from Oklahoma on account of my car plates. He was touring the state, visiting relatives with a girlfriend who was from San Diego.

'Not too keen on most of the people out here, they're kind of taut city types. Back in Texas they're more friendly, give you the time of day.'

Travelling seemed to be part of the fabric of the country. Everyone seems to have come from somewhere else. California is a state from somewhere else.

'Lived down in Tucson for twenty years but been living here for going on twelve.'

'I'm originally from Baltimore but my grandparents were Norwegian.'

'Hey are you Irish ? I've got a cousin from Cork.'

It's a country consciously aware of its own mobility and constantly interested in itself. Its sheer size, coupled with the immediacy of its own liquid history, force it to grasp the local, the instant. Tomorrow is somewhere else. Foreign news does not feature on the communication highway unless it has a direct American interest. Most Americans are descended from migrants but the memory is more recent than that.

It is a country from nowhere and everywhere. A country that has such a huge effect on the rest of the world and is not even aware of it. The world wants in but America goes on regardless.

Fear and Faith

I was asked for money in Fresno. I had stopped at a gas station for another ten dollars of fuel and eighty cents of coke. It was mid-afternoon; the sun was bright and the forecourt simmered. A young man appeared at the side of the car, hand outstretched, catching me as I turned to unlock the petrol cap.

'Got any dollars,' he mouthed. His eyes gazed,

focusing slowly. 'My car's broken down. I need some dough.' The sounds slurred out of his mouth, half-formed and stained with the smell of cheap alcohol.

He didn't threaten me; just asked.

I dug in my pocket for a couple of notes. I usually give money to people who ask but I could see the news reports; a quick couple of seconds. Then a move on. Another brief tragedy lost to the airwaves.

The man smiled, black skin glistening, then edged away, three dollars richer for a question.

Coursing through the channels in a cheap motel room on the edge of Gallup there's a news item on a couple of German tourists held up in a rest area in the hills outside Los Angeles.

They had stopped to admire the view down into the hazy valley. The sun was dropping quickly way out over the Pacific. Other couples doing the same, spread out between the empty spaces.

A Dodge pulls up filled with three men. Young men, intent on robbery and used to violence.

The Germans are obviously foreign; something sets them apart. Money is demanded and refused. The men fire and take what they had asked for, then move.

The scene is viewed from the air in a channel 9, scene-of-incident helicopter. The thick beating of the propellers against air saturates the immediacy of live commentary. The police helicopter flashes past. Ambulances and flashing cars cordon the scene of crime a few hundred feet below. The camera scans the rest area; a body is visible, face down, shape contorted: lifeless. The woman is dead, her husband is in a critical condition. The announcement ends with a general warning for tourists to avoid unknown areas and only to stay in reputable hotels. Don't walk after dark. Followed by general comments on how such incidents harm tourism.

Then the item is finished; the screen returns to a bland studio; moving onto further coverage of the election issues.

No more of the Germans. Nothing of grieving families, the expectation of travel and anticipation of return. All cut down. No flight back to Frankfurt on a Lufthansa filled with stories of football and the Grand Canyon. All lost on the fickle throw of chance. How many other routes ? A change of plan, minor delays, another coffee, a day longer in Vegas, added to a couple of Germans being in a rest-area overlooking Los Angeles on a warm Tuesday evening in July. Any change and nothing.

Fate doesn't scare me. I don't believe in fate. Chance is too believable. Sudden death scares me.

Fate only becomes fate once it has happened. Fate is never the future, only the past. Chance is the future.

Travelling throws open the doors of chance. A chance beyond the normal rhythms of living. And it is chance not danger but danger may accompany it closer.

I'm sitting in a room surrounded by people. It's a big room and the people attend to business of their own. Moving around, sharing tables, comfortably air-conditioned from heat and reality. A handful look dangerous, capable of being on the edge or are already falling. Free falling down.

I begin to sweat. The crush of people. The deluge of overwhelming information. A panic attack in Bakersfield library. I must be drinking too much coffee. I need to leave.

Retreating to the car, I ease into its comforting redness, deep and soothing. Perhaps the Japanese designed it that way. After a couple of blocks I'm calm again. The car is running smooth and low to the concrete. The click of rubber over the cracks is regular and reassuring. I drive north, away from the fear, along 99 to Fresno.

Who's Listening to Garth ?

Running late to reach Salinas, I try sleeping in the car. Hidden by a vineyard I guess I'm safe until the morning.

The trip's fragmenting. I've lost the road and wander aimlessly around the San Joaquin valley. I'm looking for an ending after the flow of the journey. The great push of manifest destiny stops in California, where the people have gone a little crazy.

The personal becomes paramount and property everything.

The search on the stereo sticks above a new radio station. It is devoted entirely to the music of Garth Brooks. Twenty-four hours a day of Garth records.

'Hell, he sure is big enough,' comments one of the DJs when questioned on the phone by a new listener on the feasibility of a monostation. I imagine what kind of people listened all day to their favourite singer. How many songs Garth had actually recorded ? At what point did they have to start playing them again? Did they have a fixed schedule or could they change the order to give their listeners a surprise ? How much in royalties was Garth getting out of it or did he own the station as an extravagant bouquet of Narcissus to himself ? Niche listening, as everyone strives to be unique.

I think I found sleep easy as Garth ploughed through some of his slow numbers.

Tipping ?

Harsh white beams flood the Honda throwing me out of sleep. An Izuzu pick-up has cornered me in the vineyard. I panic, slithering for the door and escape. The lights change to flashing blue and red: the adrenalin in my blood fades. I guess the police are not going to rob me.

The cop is huge, with a gun fixed tight on his holster. I'm on private property and will have to move. I remember little of the drive as I push back onto the freeway at 3 a.m.

Heading west again I cross I-5 then the Diablo range which rise smooth and dry from the valley base before stopping at a roadhouse at six, a few miles short of Salinas. It is already busy.

A waitress grudgingly shows me to a table. I've been driving all night and look rough but I've got money to pay.

A breakfast of hash browns, toast and eggs arrives with a grimace. She has decided I'm not going to give her a tip. An hour later, on a refilled caffeine high, I offer to pay the bill by Visa. The waitress informs me through clenched teeth there's no space on the Visa for service.

A week later I'm drinking in a bar called Vesuvio on the North Shore of San Francisco. I'm waiting for a flight and the car has gone. Time is slow but San Francisco is a city filled with books and references. The beer is easy and delivered to the table by a smiling blonde girl. I give her a tip on my second order but because it's hidden in a sheaf of dollars that might just cover the bill she assumes I never gave her one.

On the way out she stands by the door. 'It's been a pleasure serving you.' Her voice is dripping with rancour as if I'm personally responsible for her working long hours in a crowded bar and by not providing a monetary gift in appreciation of this sacrifice I've committed an unforgivable personal insult.

In America you can get as much pleasant service as you can pay for. Nobody wants to serve you because you're actually in a bar or a café because it's a good place to be, they want to serve you only if you can provide them with some compensation for their time and effort. If not, you're way down on the c-list. This striving for service is government encouraged through the taxing of tips expected to have been received. Therefore if no tip is offered they're getting taxed on money never received, which makes them really happy. However if you've got money to burn, people will kiss your ass for a slice of it; make sure if you're giving it, you're giving it obviously, so they can have an opportunity to be real grateful. Or am I being cynical?

The wages are the minimum and below. There's no culture of being paid well for working the rough shifts. Tips can be the only source of significant income for many serving staff. This is not happy employment. Another side. Always another side.

There was a sign in the bar under a framed note of a dollar bill. The words read the legend: 'Actual tip from an Australian tourist.'

I like the Aussies; they've got the right idea. Get paid for what you're doing and get paid fair.

> *'This country's as free as you got jack to pay for it.'*
> *The Grapes of Wrath*

Looking for Steinbeck

I'd read the books and the man had shifted. You can know too much about an author. Steinbeck knew that and had first avoided the publicity that had come with his success but it caught him. Thick biographies analysing his every move and critical reference pour out of over-funded American universities. Scholarly theses on the meaning of a turtle flipped off the gun metal road by a truck. People will write because they can. But I was in Salinas and nothing but my writing had got me there.

Salinas was the small farming town he had grown up in as a boy, providing many of the characters who coloured his stories. He would live to hate and love the town again. His ashes are scattered over a family plot in a graveyard called the Garden of Memories on the southern side of town.

I arrived on a Sunday morning, one year early for the planned visitor center which was being financed by the Steinbeck Foundation. Salinas was as slow as Bakersfield but looked older. New development seemed to have missed it completely. The buildings put up in a rush of enthusiasm that stopped abruptly with the Depression and didn't seem to get started again.

There was a shopping mall and a parking lot named after him. A waiter in the obligatory coffee bar reckoned he'd been run out of town in the 'thirties in some dispute with the town mayor and newspaper proprietor. There was a dark roast bearing his name. Refills were half-price.

The house he had grown up in is on Central Avenue. It is owned by the Valley Guild who serve gourmet lunches to visiting groups. Their interest in cooking is the main function of the house but its historical connections give it a useful selling point. All profits from the lunches are donated to charity.

'Eighty-one guild members raised $80,000 over 49 days in a valley-wide fund drive in order to restore and preserve this fine Salinas Valley landmark.'

They print a leaflet which gives details of serving times and strange idiosyncratic details of the author's childhood and family relations. Esther Steinbeck Rogers was married on the landing at the base of the stairs.

There are no weekend lunches but I'm allowed to look around. A sad picture of a brother and sister on top of a pony stare out from a frame above the main dining room.

The house is empty but curiously untouched. I wonder what happened to all the people? I guess they grew old and died.

'Nobody but nobody knows what's going to happen to anybody beside the forlorn rags of growing old.'
Jack Kerouac

The Lady in the Blue Suit

An image keeps appearing of a woman in a blue suit and late middle age. She's a success, a symbol, and people like her here. At a banquet she is fêted, told how successful, how clever, how right. She begins to believe.

At first she asks about sickness. But look around you, they say, there's no sickness here and if you are there's insurance.

But what if you're poor ? she asks. Look around you, they say, everyone can afford; everyone's rich here.

And she looks and there's no-one sick or poor at the banquet.

Later she's being driven by a black man in a limousine. Because he's a good driver and she's going to be rich. On her ride home she believes. This is the future. She can't feel the heat or cracked concrete of the freeway underneath.

The city was fine. I had nowhere to go but hang around and catch a Greyhound to LAX. How do you end a journey? Check in, fly home.